PIECES TO PURPOSE

UNBREAKABLE WOMEN WHO REFUSED TO GIVE UP

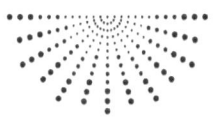

ALICIA RAFFKIND   ANGELINA SMITH

CARRIE KASS   DEANNA COX

DEBORAH OWEN VALENTINE

DR. HOLLY NOEL BROCATO   DR. CINDY STEWARD

JULIE SMITH   LISABETH THOMAS   MARY PARKER

MEG HAYS   MELINDA GARVEY   NATASHA CAMPISI

REBECCA ANNE PRICE   SAMANTHA MCCOY

THERESA PORE   VANESSA GARCIA

CONTENTS

SULIT PRESS

Ready to fast-track your publishing career, increase your visibility, or boost your business?

Harness the power of partnership by contributing a 3,000-word chapter to one of our upcoming Multi-Author Books!

If you are...
☑ Inspired by what you do and want to generously share what you've learned...
☑ Committed to meeting deadlines and doing your best work...
☑ Ready to connect with other aspiring authors who are as excited as you are to share your book with the world...
Then our Multi-Author Book might be the right path for you! Learn more at sulitpress.com

INTRODUCTION

"Be kind, for everyone you meet is fighting a hard battle." – Ian MacLaren

The word *empathy* has grown in popularity in recent years, along with an emerging awareness that we all might fare a little better if we took a moment to put ourselves in someone else's shoes. This can be a challenging exercise for even the most compassionate among us, but the real obstacle to seeing the world through someone else's perspective is that we rarely have the foggiest clue what they have been through.

Shame, regret, fear of judgment, and a desire to let "dead dogs lie" keep women quiet about their darkest truths. But when those moments are brought into the light, as the brave authors have

done in this book, something magical happens—
real healing begins.

Pieces to Purpose is not just a collection of stories;
it's a testament to the human spirit's resilience.
Each of the seventeen chapters is a raw,
unapologetic dive into a world where life does
not hand out easy answers. These stories are
often unsettling, yet they shine with hope. The
authors pull back the curtain on life experiences
many of us only hear about in whispers, if at all.
Here, we find narratives of surviving rape and
domestic abuse, overcoming hidden addictions,
and stepping into unimaginable roles to support
family and self. We meet women who have
wrestled with their identities, struggled through
heart-wrenching losses, and battled silent wars
with their own fears and doubts.

What unites these stories is the transformation
each author found on the other side of her trials.
These aren't merely tales of survival; they're
powerful journeys of self-discovery, strength,
and, ultimately, purpose. In facing their personal
mountains, each of these women has emerged
with a newfound sense of meaning that
transcends her individual experiences. Their
stories remind us that we are not alone in our

pain, nor are we alone in our capacity to heal and rebuild.

For every woman whose story graces these pages, the path has been fraught with hardship, yet the courage to speak up and speak out turns her experiences into a guiding light for others. This book serves as both a mirror and a map—reflecting the pain we've known in ourselves or in others and guiding us to find meaning, strength, and purpose through our own adversities.

We hope that as you turn each page, you'll find moments of connection, empathy, and even transformation. These women's journeys were not easy, but their willingness to share them has created a safe space where wounds can find healing, shame can be shed, and strength can be rediscovered.

May *Pieces to Purpose* remind you that, no matter the depths of your own story, there is light to be found, healing to be embraced, and purpose to be uncovered.

ACCIDENT-PRONE

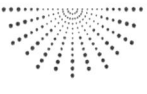

MEG HAYS

*a*s a newly graduated third-grader, I race across the green lawn, my stringy blonde hair flying behind me. The faded, hand-me-down t-shirt hangs loosely on my tiny frame, and my pink plastic flip-flops hug my feet as I dash through the yard.

I'm off to my best friend's house to celebrate the last day of the school year.

The air carries a pungent smell of freshly mowed grass, and my mind is already spinning with excitement about days to come filled with swimming pool shenanigans, softball practice—where I won't be able to hit the ball to save my life—and dozens of sleepovers with friends in the neighborhood.

I giggle with anticipation because summer has always been my favorite. Sweat begins to bead on my forehead as I sprint around the corner.

Nothing could be more perfect than this moment. Life feels like it is just beginning, and I can't imagine a more idyllic day than this one.

Then I step off the curb.

Why can't I catch my breath? I must be dreaming because I'm pretty sure I am lying down, which means I am nestled in my ginormous double bed.

I love my new bed, especially since I got my own room after Kelly married. Lucky me, right? Well, except for the old, faded, patchwork carpet. But Mom promised I could get a pink carpet soon. Pink is Kimberly's favorite color.

Wait, Kimberly? Where's Kimberly? Wasn't I running to her house?

"Oh, crap! My neck hurts." *Mommy would be proud I said crap instead this time. But where is Mommy?*

"Mommy? Where is my Mommy? I want my Mommy! MOMMY!"

Is that my voice? I can't breathe. My voice sounds funny. Why can't I breathe? Ouch! What is pressing into my neck? Is that gravel digging into my back?

"Are you okay? Can you get up? Where do you live? Oh, shit! Hey! Hey! Don't pass out on me!"

Turns out, the last day of third grade wasn't perfect. In fact, for years, I would say that day ruined my life.

As I stepped off the curb, a fifteen-year-old boy on a ten-speed bike crashed into me.

We both tumbled to the asphalt, and his six-foot body fell on top of my three-foot frame while the handlebars of the bicycle jammed into my neck, crushing my esophagus.

That poor teenager carried my limp body to the closest house. My house.

Terrified and shocked by the sight of my listless body, my sixteen-year-old sister Heather scooped me up in her arms and jumped in the passenger seat of my mom's car. At the same time, Mom scooted into the driver's seat to tear out of the driveway and drove like a bat out of hell to the emergency room. To their horror, I stopped breathing while Heather held my small body, which lay battered and bruised.

Worst last day of school EVER!

Fuzzy memories still replay in my mind of a team of doctors surrounding me, urgently working to open my collapsed airways. Miraculously, my esophagus sustained no long-term harmful effects. After a quick procedure in the ER, I was sent home that evening with no further treatment except the instructions for my parents to watch me for brain swelling due to the concussion.

No bones were broken, and the only outward scars were from the stitches required on my chin from the handlebars and my right knee from the bike pedals.

Hallelujah!

However, the injuries to my soul took years to heal.

"Mom said she wasn't going to ask you again to take a bite of your cheeseburger," Daddy announced as he slipped into his chair at the head of the table.

He'd just gotten home from a long day at his print shop in the city and was late to dinner, like usual. My two other sisters had already finished and had been excused from the table. Oh, how I wished I could be with them.

Tears welled up in my eyes as I nervously shifted in my chair at the dinner table and stared at that stupid cheeseburger on my plate.

Didn't they see the nibble of bread I took on the left side? Didn't they know that bite was still hanging in my throat, and I couldn't seem to swallow it down?

It had already been another long evening rooted to the seat, begging God to make my mom's home-cooked meal disappear.

Uh-oh, it was happening again. My throat was tightening up, and I couldn't breathe. My already sweaty hands began to fidget in my lap. Didn't Daddy realize I couldn't swallow and my throat was closing as he spoke?

I knew better than to argue with my dad, and even though I was pretty sure I would die this time, I also realized I better hurry up and say something. So, I coughed to clear my throat and responded to my dad's prompting.

"Daddy, like I told Mommy, I already ate pizza at Kimberly's house earlier. I'm not hungry," I lied, with my eyes glued to my sweaty hands.

He was not buying it.

One thing was for sure: I was about to be punished again for not eating my dinner for the umpteenth time.

Oh, how I wished I could eat food like a normal person.

Damp leaves, twigs, and gravel clung to my tattered Camp Timberlee T-shirt as I crawled and hoisted myself out of the ten-foot ravine. My arm, which laid awkwardly and limp on my right side, was not helping the climb.

Slowly, my gaze focused across the narrow, tree-lined country road to the Honda 90 motorcycle haphazardly balancing on its side. The back wheel rotated steadily as if trying to put me into a trance.

Movement grabbed my attention to my left, and I gaped dumbly at my sister, Heather, running away.

A scream caught in my throat as I attempted to pursue her. My legs buckled beneath me, and I fell to my knees. Heather jerked around as if she heard my silent scream and yelled, "Stay there, Meg! I'm going to get help!"

"Don't leave me! Please! Don't leave me!"

My eyes closed, and I licked my chapped lips. I took a breath.

Whew, I didn't seem to be choking, but I had no idea where I was or what was happening. I needed to rest for a minute before I hurried after Heather so I wouldn't be alone, but I couldn't find the energy to stand back up.

I might be dying this time.

"Surgery went well, Mr. and Mrs. Morgan," said the man in blue scrubs and a funny-looking cloth cap covering his head. "Meg did fine. She's a strong little girl, but the compound fracture will take at least three months to heal. We can take the pin out where the arm snapped in half at that time. I would feel more comfortable if you stayed in the area instead of heading back to Chicago so soon after the accident. She might miss the first week or two of school...fifth grade, right?"

Mom nodded, glanced toward me, and smiled

through the tears of relief that hadn't stopped trickling down her face.

"The nurse will bring a glass of water and two Tylenol on her next round. That should help keep your daughter comfortable as the anesthesia wears off," the doctor added as he headed toward the door.

My mind glommed onto his words. *Two Tylenol. Umm...no, thank you. I can't swallow pills.*

The familiar sweat began to gather on my palms and my breathing quickened.

At least I could attempt to chew my food well enough to swallow, but now, I would have to swallow a hard pill without chewing, and on purpose? There was no way that would happen.

Here we go again.

* * *

Adolescence and teenage years flew by, except for breakfast, lunch, and, worst of all, the dreaded dinner hour. However, as I matured, I mastered my magician skills, learning to discreetly cough any food that felt like a choking hazard into the napkin on my lap.

Abracadabra! All gone.

I sure wish it was that easy.

The sound of the grandfather clock in the foyer striking the nightly six o'clock hour echoed in my mind as the air suddenly thickened, my hands burst into an oozing river of sweat, and my tongue turned into a parched, swollen, thick, and hard rock in my mouth.

Dear God, please let Mom deviate from her standard dinnertime ritual and decide she and Daddy need a date night at the country club.

My fingertips were already tingling.

* * *

The Memphis State University campus was bustling with thousands of students speeding through the narrow streets, headed toward the roads leading out of town to start the weekend.

I couldn't wait to get home to see my boyfriend, Lee, considering it had already felt like a decade since Christmas vacation ended. I had to leave him behind when I returned to Memphis to start the second semester of my junior year in college.

It'd been a rough month since the holiday break. The panic attacks were rearing their ugly heads more often, becoming increasingly frequent, and lasting exponentially longer. This meant I couldn't eat if Lee wasn't around.

Lee made me feel safe and never questioned why I ate like a bird. Plus, he didn't judge me when I suggested we swing by Kroger for a gallon of ice cream—as long as it had nothing chunky that might get stuck in my throat.

As I entered the on-ramp to Interstate Forty, I recognized the familiar tightening of my chest as I looked at the half-empty Pepsi can between my legs. My mouth began to feel parched like it always did before I descended into one of my "bid for attention episodes." That's what Mom called it when I heard her whispering to Dad about my last rant over the holidays about leaving me alone regarding not eating dinner.

Note to self: Only wear my roommate Lindsey's oversized Guess sweatshirt in front of Mom this weekend. Maybe it would hide my five-foot-two and eighty-six-pound figure. If she caught a glimpse of my emaciated body, she was going to freak out and once again threaten to take me to the doctor for a feeding tube.

I rolled down the window to let the cold air in and maybe dilute the thick oxygen that I couldn't seem to breathe in quick enough or deep enough into my lungs. My hands were already tingling, and sweat dripped down my bony back.

Was my heart racing fast enough for a heart attack? A pain behind my eyes was beginning to thump methodically. I was probably having a stroke. I almost wish I was. At least then, someone would listen to me that there was something genuinely wrong with me.

I chugged down the last drops of Pepsi and realized I had no more drinks in my car.

How could I be so stupid? I knew better than to leave home without a six-pack of soda in my little travel cooler. I'd only make it to my parent's house if I gulped down carbonated drinks to calm myself and make sure my throat stayed open. The burn of the soda bubbles traveling down my esophagus always assured me that nothing was stuck and I was not strangling.

Uh oh. Here it goes.

My vision blurred, but I could see the Exit Fourteen sign ahead.

Dear Lord, please let me make it. Oh, God! Please make this panic stop! What is wrong with me? Why am I like this? Everyone says it's all in my head, but I can't STOP IT! This is crazy! Oh, God, my worst fear...DO NOT LET ME BE CRAZY!

"The Lord is my Shepherd, I shall not want..."

Ok, Meg. Just take this exit. You can do it. You're getting close. I can see the pay phone from here. Just get out and make it to the phone. You can do this. Call Mom. Call Mom. Call Mom. She'll know what to do.

Please let Mom be at the office. I need to talk to her, but I won't be able to if she's already gone home because the toll-free calls only work at the office. Please, God, please let her answer the phone!

* * *

"I understand, but we have to do something. It took her six hours and ten phone calls to make it home from Memphis. Jim, you know that drive only takes two and a half hours. Something is wrong. Look at her. She's skin and bones. I don't know what to do anymore. She won't eat. You have to help her." Mom was urgently whispering to our family doctor outside the patient room I was sitting in.

I was exhausted. I felt like I'd been hit by a bus.

The good news was that I felt so much better now that I was with my mom. The bad news was that Mom and Dad were going to be pissed all weekend because of the drama I caused over the past six hours, struggling to make the drive home. Maybe I should have just stayed at school this weekend.

"Okay, Meg," the doctor started as he entered the room, with Mom shuffling close behind him. "We have gone through this before. There is nothing wrong with you. There is nothing wrong with your throat or esophagus, and there is nothing wrong, period."

The older gentleman in his crisp white coat stared at me for what felt like ages and continued, "You need to stop this nonsense and be grateful you don't have real health issues. This is all in your head. Don't you see how much this hurts your mom and dad?"

Great. I have heard this before, and my greatest fear is confirmed. I. AM. CRAZY.

"So, if it's all in my head, why can't you open my head and fix it?" I said under my breath. No one heard me, though. The doctor was already holding the door so my mom could leave the room.

* * *

Like the polite, young woman I'd been raised to be, I navigated the world desperately trying to hide the chaos I felt inside, pretending I was not the head case I feared I was.

The tether to my sanity was running thin and I didn't think I could continue the perception that I was ok for very much longer.

The office of the first psychiatrist appointment of my life was much smaller than I had imagined. I was twenty-seven-years-old and struggling to continue the facade of "having my shit together." My nerves felt like they were running on the outside of my skin at all times and I stressed daily about what I could eat that would keep me from the feeling of choking. Most mornings I wanted to stay in bed.

My sick days were depleting, and I was pretty

sure Lee was beginning to wonder why I always wanted to be glued to his side.

As of yet, he didn't fully understand when I told him I felt like I was going crazy because I was fearful of choking all the time. Poor guy. He definitely married a basket case and I got the sense he was starting to realize it.

This appointment better go well. My sanity and my marriage depended on it.

"Meg Hays?" the tall, blonde woman holding the door open called into the waiting room.

This was it. Please, God—let her give me something, anything that would help. Just don't let it be a pill. I can't swallow those.

* * *

Why did my body ache all over? I couldn't seem to take a full, deep breath. Every inch from head to toe was screaming in pain, and I felt like I'd collided with a bullet train.

What was happening? Was I dreaming of the bicycle accident again? Where was I? Was this real? Wake up, Meg!

Oh, wait. It was coming back to me. I was definitely not dreaming. I was hit...but it was by a car this time. One moment I was exiting the parked car and the next thing I knew, I was on the ground because the car was not actually in park.

What was with me and vehicles? A bicycle, motorcycle, and now a freaking car? What the ever-loving hell?

As I laid in my bed, battered and bruised from being hit by a car in the driveway, I had a weird sense of déjà vu, and something shifted inside of me.

No more. Absolutely. No. More.

I was done faking it. I was done living in fear. I was done feeling like a freak. Honestly, more than anything else, I was done pretending that something wasn't wrong.

At forty-seven years old, it was long overdue to face what had plagued me since I was eight. The fears, the anxiety that constantly hummed through my veins, and the panic attacks that knocked me flat on my ass had never left me alone for long, and it was time I did something about them.

That day, I decided to loosen the tightly wound noose of fear and anxiety. I would not remain a victim. I might not have all the answers yet, but I was committed to making changes until I discovered what worked.

It was time to focus on healing—for myself, my family, and my future.

Dear God, You haven't removed my panic and anxiety, so I'm asking for something different: the strength and courage to face whatever lies ahead. I am weak, but You are strong. I need Your help, Your guidance, and maybe a few flashing neon signs to direct my steps.

I surrender. Please don't leave me—I can't do this alone.

At 20 pounds overweight, I was tired of being exhausted, depressed, anxiety-ridden, and miserable. My marriage was unraveling, my kids were suffering from my mental absence, and I'd lost all passion for living a purposeful life.

Most mornings, I didn't even want to get out of bed. I dreamt of staying snuggled under the covers, binge-watching Hallmark Christmas movies in the dark for hours, or until I needed to use the restroom—whichever came first.

Despite the fact I had been on anxiety medication since I was twenty-seven, it had never been enough. At any moment, I knew I could be at the mercy of heart palpitations, sweaty palms, a lump in my throat, or tingly fingertips.

If I was to defeat this beast, I knew I was in for significant life changes and intense counseling sessions. I was positive this process was going to hurt, but surely it couldn't be any worse than the wounds I had been racking up since I was a third grader.

My hand felt for my phone on the bedside table. I picked it up, and through swollen eyes, I dialed the therapist's number.

Those first three months of counseling were the most difficult. As I slowly began to process my childhood trauma, my present struggles, and everything in between, I began to understand how my feelings of safety had been hijacked along the way.

The sessions were long, tear-filled, and sometimes torturous, as I would relive moments of pain and loneliness. Many times, I would leave my therapist's office completely drained and worthless for the rest of the day.

Wasn't that what I was trying to fix?

The answer was yes, but these old wounds would take time to heal. They were black, indelible marks of unworthiness, weakness, and doom-laden fear etched on my soul that I had never wanted to face before.

Around the same time, I consulted a former coworker who had become a health coach. Her health program was a game-changer, and my weight was one of the things I needed to work on due to the enormous amounts of nutrient-deficient, soft, processed foods I had eaten most of my life.

The program focused on nutrition as the key to change and better habit creation. As I ate more nutritious food, a profound shift began to happen, not just in my weight but also in my mental health.

Nearly five years into eating the healthiest I'd ever eaten, I continued to see a massive improvement in my mental health, my ability to manage panic disorder, and even my fear of choking.

And guess what? On those high-anxiety days when I felt the lump in my throat begin to emerge, I learned I can blend, mash, or stir anything I need to—and that's okay.

Additionally, the stringy, blonde-haired girl from long ago was well-loved. When she came out scared and anxious, I was there to hug her, love her, and remind her that God was the one who gave her strength and courage.

No longer was I begging for God to take away the anxiety, but instead to show me what my body is trying to tell me. Do I need to slow down? Eat better? Talk to someone? Or maybe focus on breathing?

Most importantly, I became an anxiety coach to support women who, like me, struggled with anxiety and eating issues and felt alone in their battles. Through compassionate guidance, I helped these women find relief by building healthy habits, uncovering self-sabotaging thoughts, and creating routines that bring peace and stability.

For so long, I felt incredibly lonely. Fear, panic, and anxiety isolated me, and I spent years disconnected from others, feeling like no one understood my struggles and that I was weird, crazy, and weak.

My accident-prone journey showed me that my past experiences were the tools I needed to reach back, connect, and guide others through a healing process of the pieces that once left us broken.

I've turned the loneliness I once felt into a mission to create a community. In this place, women can come together, support one another, encourage each other, and grow in faith as we work toward healthier lives. God, indeed, can use our pieces for His purpose.

My healing journey was far from perfect, but one thing I learned without a doubt: the things I allow into my body, mind, and spirit matter more than anything else I do for my health, much less life.

Like a vehicle, if I fuel it with the best gasoline, it will run like a beast. But if I pour sugar into the tank, it will break down before I leave the driveway.

That's precisely what food, scripture, prayer, and people do for me. I can't effectively deal with life and the situations within without fueling myself with quality ingredients to help me run at my best.

Especially since I might need to be on the lookout for a bus or train headed my way!

I can now see how those "accidents" were blessings in disguise because they equipped me to help others manage their own anxiety well. Without my pieces, I would not have been able to fulfill a much-needed purpose.

MEG HAYS

Meg Hays is an anxiety coach, speaker, and best-selling author who loves nothing more than helping women kick anxiety to the curb and step into a life of wellness. With her years of experience in health coaching and her own journey of panic disorder, Meg brings a fun, faith-filled and holistic approach to managing anxiety well: focusing on the powerful combination of nutrition, mindset, healthy habits, and community support. As the founder of Meg Hays Healthy Living and the Live Well Community, Meg is on a mission to help women ditch those anxiety-ridden days, sleepless nights, and those dreaded panic attacks. She believes that real change comes from small, simple steps and powerful mindset shifts—all within a supportive community. Through her dynamic coaching programs, engaging talks, and inspiring writing, Meg encourages women to live their healthiest, most vibrant lives by choosing to live well, every day.

www.meghays.com
https://www.facebook.com/meg.hays
https://www.instagram.com/meghays72/
https://www.linkedin.com/in/meg-morgan-hays/

2

RECLAIMING JUSTICE

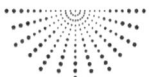

SAMANTHA MCCOY

"*There* is no justice in the justice system." These words are forever seared into my memory. *How could this be true?* I wondered. I couldn't understand a system set up to protect perpetrators and harm the victims of crime. Yet, as I stood in that parking lot hearing my attorney make that statement, I knew—profoundly and personally—just how right he was.

College was an incredible experience. Each semester brought me closer to my dream of becoming a mental health therapist. However, I never imagined my undergraduate journey would be destroyed so close to my senior year.

Raped and beaten, I faced a decision that night whether to report to law enforcement. This choice is difficult for any victim of rape, but in my case, an additional paralyzing fear held me back: The rapist was a city police officer. Reporting a crime so deeply violating to his colleagues, or worse, having to face him in the station, was a horrifying thought. But how could I sleep knowing he might return to harm me again —or hurt someone else? An unexplainable urge compelled me to report.

Led into a cold interrogation room barely larger than a closet, I took in the cramped space—a tiny table and a few chairs. After what felt like hours, an officer finally entered. Overwhelmed, I felt a confusing sense of relief mixed with fear. *Was he the rapist's friend? Can I trust him?* Summoning every ounce of courage, I poured out every painful detail. A surge of relief washed over me, thinking the worst of the reporting process was behind me.

Oh, how I wish that had been the case.

Surprisingly, a new officer entered, and I was asked to repeat what happened.

To my horror, I repeated the details of the attack at least five times. Emotionally exhausted and still covered in injuries, I poured my heart out. Each repetition felt like a small piece of my soul was stripped away.

Late into the night, I was told we needed to go to the emergency room. Like a zombie, and with nothing left inside, I was escorted by two officers. *This will all be over soon*, I told myself. *They just want to ensure I'm physically okay.*

The nurse entered with no expression, immediately informing me that a rape kit would be taken, and handed me two pills. Confused, I asked what they were for. She flatly stated they were for preventing sexually transmitted diseases and pregnancy. Until that moment, I hadn't considered the possibility of either. Disease? Pregnancy? I was so broken.

Exhaustion overwhelmed me, layered with suffocating anxiety, yet I was numb. I had to disrobe so the nurse could photograph my injuries. I wanted to crawl out of my skin. My body no longer felt like my own. It was a crime scene—probed, photographed, inspected.

The rest of that awful hospital visit is a blank in my memory. My mind must have shut down, protecting me from more pain.

Around three a.m., two officers came to my hospital room and told me we had to go to the crime scene so I could show them where the rape occurred. All I wanted was for the night to end, to stop reliving the attack, to sleep, and never wake up. But there I was, standing in the room where the rape happened, showing officers in uniform where one of their own had violated me. Huddled near the door, I trembled, hands shaking, tears welling in my eyes.

Finally, they called it a night. One officer informed me I needed to return to the station by seven a.m., even though it was already four a.m. Did they not realize how much I needed to be alone? It was as though I was expected to be superhuman, to bury my pain and help solve their case without emotion. But I am only human.

As I lay in bed, my thoughts were relentless. *Embarrassment? But why?* I knew logically I had no reason to feel ashamed. I was the one attacked. Still, the thought crept in: *Had I looked at him? Had I spoken to him? Maybe things would have been different. Was I not worthy of respect?*

Before I knew it, the sun was peeking through the window. Exhausted, I returned to the police station, dreading what awaited me. *What more could they possibly need? I have already given them everything.*

Walking into the station, I held a faint hope that the officers would tell me my rapist had been arrested. But as I was led back to another interrogation room, an unfamiliar officer asked me to repeat what happened.

For the first time, frustration overwhelmed my numbness. *What do I need to say for someone to listen?* I felt like I was screaming into a void, desperately pleading for protection.

Shortly after, an officer told me I needed to wiretap the perpetrator and get him to admit to raping me. *Excuse me?* They wanted me to call the man who had assaulted me and get him to confess without any guidance on how to do it. My heart sank, terror sweeping over me. Yet I reminded myself that they were trying to help me, that I needed to step up to get justice.

So, I called.

With officers sitting behind me, I listened to the phone ring. Terrified, I prayed he wouldn't answer, but my prayer went unanswered. As his voice came through, I began to cry and asked if he had used protection during the assault. He said no. Disgusted, I couldn't bear to hear his voice any longer. I hung up, expecting some acknowledgment from the officers—a nod, a word of encouragement, anything. Instead, it was silent. Finally, one officer remarked, "It's still a 'he said, she said' case."

What? The man I told them I did not consent to had just admitted to not using protection, essentially acknowledging the act. But as I was learning, my word meant nothing against his.

As I was escorted back to the interrogation room, we passed my mother in the waiting area. I reached for her, seeking comfort, but the officer quickly insisted I return. Trembling, I asked if my mother could join me. "No," he barked. I was left to relive the attack, alone and frightened.

They asked for my phone for a forensic examination. *Why did I feel like a suspect? Was the rapist's phone undergoing the same scrutiny?*

Numb and exhausted, I fell into a dark void over the following weeks. I lost my job, my apartment, my motivation. A friend finally convinced me to see a therapist. Once again, I recounted the rape, praying it would be the last time. The therapist's gentle, attentive look was the first semblance of compassion I had received. After listening, she said, "I'm so sorry for what you've been through. I believe you, and you deserve better." I broke down, overwhelmed by her kindness—a kindness I hadn't felt from anyone else since that night. This was the first step toward healing.

Weeks later, I was called to retrieve my phone. At the station, another officer questioned my dating app use and asked if I "liked it rough." The rapist, it seemed, had used this excuse to explain my injuries. Horrified and insulted, I stormed out. Just before I left, they threatened that I would be arrested for filing a false report if I were lying.

Rage filled me. They had no intention of helping me. They weren't investigating the rapist. They were investigating me, trying to force me into silence.

That summer, I started an internship at a law firm. When a partner asked about my stress, I finally confided in him. He offered to help, giving me a paid position. Months passed with no word on my case. Then, one day, police officers appeared at my office, unsettling my co-workers. My boss intervened, and in a private room, the officers informed us there was a video of the rape, though it was "unretrievable." How, then, did they know its contents?

Their question burned in my memory: "If you were unconscious, how did you know you didn't consent?" *Is this real?* I had to prove I didn't consent while unconscious. A video of the rape was not enough to establish my lack of consent.

I was done.

I left that room ready to raise hell. Naïve to think law enforcement would investigate another officer fairly, I now saw the truth. It was a ruse.

Time and time again, law enforcement showed up at my workplace, intimidating me with their presence, loitering by my car, and harassing me with calls. My attorney advised a civil lawsuit to bring public attention to the issue.

After gathering the necessary records, I approached the hospital to obtain my medical file. The hospital later claimed the "camera was not working" the night they photographed my injuries. My attorneys discovered that police had taken the originals, leaving no record behind.

An unknown caller finally informed me that due to "insufficient evidence," criminal charges would not proceed. I was crushed. I lost myself in self-harm, alcohol, and reckless behaviors. Trying to make myself unattractive, I binged on food, believing it might protect me. My dreams of becoming a mental health therapist faded. I was broken, unrecognizable to myself.

Although I eventually succeeded in a Title IX hearing, which banned him from campus property, and obtained a civil protective order preventing him from contacting me or coming near me, he remained an officer for approximately eleven months after the assault. One day, as I walked into the law firm, my attorney and boss informed me that he had been forced to resign quietly. I felt elated in one breath, but in the next, I was horrified and afraid he would seek revenge.

To escape the pain and terror, I decided to move across the country. It wasn't worth risking his wrath, and I certainly did not trust law enforcement to protect me, given how they had completely failed me when I initially reported. I went through the motions of graduate school in a town far from where I had been mistreated. I had escaped, yet the pain followed. I completed my Master's degree, specializing in trauma-informed practice. I buried my feelings and went on to obtain my license as a mental health therapist. Day by day, breath by breath, I repeated to myself to just take the next step in front of me. This is how I lived for three years.

Working as a therapist brought me comfort. Helping others was a beautiful distraction from my pain, and it made me feel as though my suffering had a purpose. As a crime victim counselor, I attended hearings with survivors in their pursuit of justice. However, week after week, I saw the same injustices and failures that had happened to me. All I could do was counsel the victims and support them emotionally. It wasn't enough. I could no longer accept the status quo we all blindly followed.

"There is no justice in the justice system."

No!

Not again.

Not another victim treated poorly. Society was failing survivors thousands of miles from the police department that failed me.

At that moment, I decided I would go to law school. How is the system meant to work? If I could find out, then maybe I could change the cycle of harm and failure for sexual assault survivors.

It didn't take long in law school to realize that the best way to make change is through legislation. Yes, the courts interpret the law, but the law itself comes from the legislative bills by which we are governed.

So, one night during my first year, I wrote down every failure I had experienced: no counselor or support during the reporting process, having to pay for my own rape kit and medical visit, being denied a copy of my police report, threats of a polygraph to intimidate me into silence...Then, I started cold-calling every representative and senator I could find. Fueled by the rage and pain I saw in each survivor's face, I called. I showed up. I knocked on doors and I refused to go away.

It took two years, but one day, I received a call from a senator. His words left me speechless. He shared that his mother had been a victim of sexual violence, and he had heard I was knocking on doors. He wanted to work with me and support the legislation. Time stood still. Was this really happening? I had been treated as less than human just a few years before; I was just a nobody.

But it was real. After testifying before the state senate and then the state house, I received a message as I sat in my law school lecture: "Congratulations! The bill was signed into law!" Speechless, tears welled up in my eyes. But this time, they were tears of hope—hope that future generations will never know the injustices so many survivors face today. Hope for a society where survivors are believed and treated with dignity. Hope that we all have the power to make a difference and do not have to accept injustice, no matter how steep the fight may seem.

"There is no justice in the justice system."

That statement is still true for far too many. But as I sit here today, I find solace in knowing the power each individual holds. We may have more battles to face, but rage knows no bounds. Hope has no bounds. Every person can help shape our society into one we are proud of. We must learn to tap into that hope when we speak out and channel our rage to persevere through each new day.

We cannot stop the fight. We will not accept the status quo.

SAMANTHA MCCOY

Recognized as a 2024 Texas Rising Star in appellate law, Samantha McCoy is an attorney, public speaker, activist, and licensed mental health therapist. Above all, her greatest honor has been raising her beautiful daughter alongside her fiercely supportive husband.

Following a sexually violent crime, Samantha dedicated her career to ensuring all gaps within the judicial system are finally closed and all survivors of sexual violence are treated in a dignified and trauma-informed manner. Samantha has successfully lobbied for and passed five laws in four states and one United Nations Resolution—all of which strengthened the rights and protections for survivors.

Samantha received her Master's in Social Work and a Certificate of Advanced Study in Trauma-Informed Practice from Syracuse University. She then obtained her Doctor of Jurisprudence from

St. Mary's University School of Law. She continues her lobbying efforts in the hope of a more just system for future generations.

https://www.linkedin.com/in/samantha-mccoy27

3

LET THE REDEEMED OF THE LORD SAY SO

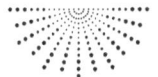

DR. HOLLY BROCATO

I was in my second failing marriage when the ground collapsed beneath me. My second husband had been inappropriate with my youngest daughter from my first marriage—a nightmare I'd only imagined in the deepest crevices of dread.

At the time, I barely had joint custody of my three children from my first marriage and this incident was not only the most sickening and frightening thing that could happen BUT it also endangered what little joint custody I was allotted after an ugly court battle. With my kids at the vulnerable ages of thirteen, ten, and seven years; I did not hesitate to leave my second husband in a state of emergency.

Jobless and desperate, I'd been scouring ads for weeks, clutching at anything, and receiving only echoes of "not this time." My resume was a list of short stints—administrative assistant, technical writer, sales assistant: I'd spun through a revolving door of jobs that didn't last. Each position evaporated like the last. And in the depths of a recession that gobbled up middle management and spat out secretaries, I found myself lost, faced with one absolute certainty; something had to change.

I was determined not to go crawling back to my parents for help, money, or a place to stay. That kind of request came with conditions, a leash I'd broken free from years ago. No. There had to be another way. I couldn't fail my children again, no matter the cost.

When I picked up the Houston Press that day, flipping to the classified section like I had a hundred times before, I thought maybe I'd find something I'd missed. There was the usual stream of uninspiring opportunities. Then, one ad stopped me in my tracks.

"Now Hiring an Assistant to Entertain Male Clientele Traveling into Town for Conferences." The ad's tone felt almost... innocuous. I told myself I'd book their flights and set up dinner reservations. My mind spun a little narrative, a desperate justification.

I met her—my prospective boss—at a sushi restaurant in the Galleria area. The moment I walked in, I felt out of place. The hostess sized me up, and based on her appearance, my Target outfit was immediately labeled "disposable" and less-than-worthy.

And then, she walked in. My boss-to-be was elegance personified. She glided through the restaurant like she belonged, capturing every gaze in the room without even a smile. She was magnetic, and every detail was perfect, from the precision of her heels to the understated confidence in her walk. When she ordered, her voice flirted with the world itself.

"Ketel One Lemon Drop Martini, please," she said, flashing a smile that somehow invited admiration and created distance.

"First, let me say," she began, her tone both casual and deliberate. "You don't have to do anything you don't want to."

I barely processed her words. My heart was a hardened, impenetrable shell dulled by years of betrayal, disrespect, and the lingering ache of children lost to a ruthless ex-husband. Under her gaze and the weight of my desperation, in that dim-lit booth, I committed. Not to a future or even to a plan, but to survival.

At first, I kept it strictly transactional; one-hour "body rubs" in a back suite, hidden away in a strip center. I stayed with a friend, lived in her guest room for a few months, and did the thing. It was strange stepping into that role, but in a way, I was good at it. Slowly, subtly, I grew bolder, the novelty of my nakedness shifting into a strange kind of armor. My body—its beauty, its vulnerability—was no longer something I hid or protected. And with that boldness came a recklessness.

It was Labor Day weekend, and we were busy with bookings. My boss was caught up in her "real job" downtown, so I was alone when the last client of the day arrived; a handsome, tall man with red hair and a quick smile. I thought he was different—he seemed down-to-earth and kind even. We talked and exchanged easy conversation, and he made me feel, if only for a moment, like a person again instead of a commodity. Then, I returned from securing the payment, and he pulled out his badge.

That should've been it—the arrest, the label "prostitute" branded across my record. I waited for the shame to descend, to feel trapped in it. But that night, as I walked out of the police station, released on a technicality by a swift-acting attorney, I didn't feel shame. Instead, a sick, embittered resolve settled in. The world had taken plenty from me. I could take this one thing back.

Let me be clear, I wasn't doe-eyed, nor did I think all would end well, and I'd marry Richard Gere. I knew the risks and chose to take them. I knew it was wrong—and did it anyway.

"What the hell?" you may say.

Yes, the world had become a fresh hell, and I would give it back all the wrong it had dealt me. What a joke. I had three beautiful children and a controlling ex-husband, and for one hour at a time, I callously used men for money.

Some might say this happens when a person doesn't find their purpose soon enough in life or that it's the result of being born from an affair and given up for adoption. But mine isn't a sob story, friends. I was a Christian when I made the worst decisions of my life. Some might say I didn't deserve all the good God blessed me with, and to them, I'd say this: When the prodigal son—or daughter—returns, a parent can't help but shower them with love beyond measure. In the Bible Rahab wasn't in the lineage of Jesus Christ because she was a "good girl." No, she was a prostitute at the walls of Jericho who led a hard life. She lived passionately and took a risk to help the Israelite spies infiltrate Jericho. For her courage, she was redeemed and God made her part of Christ's lineage. While there are so many choices I regret, God has redeemed me too.

I was blessed to be adopted and brought home on my father's 30th birthday. I was the ultimate gift to a couple who couldn't conceive—a better baby no one could find, loved beyond measure, with my only flaw being separation anxiety. (Could you blame me? I was given up for adoption two weeks before I was born.) But I had a good life. Product of divorce? Yes—but that was no excuse for the adulteress I'd become. God Himself was the only one who could see past my poor choices and form a diamond from coal.

Some might think, "She doesn't seem apologetic or convicted of her wrongdoings." There were close calls. Once, before a family therapy session where I feared my secret might be revealed, I asked my ex-husband if he'd gotten calls from people trying to ruin my life. He replied calmly, "Some definitely called to hurt you, but most cared about you and just wanted you to stop before you got hurt." For that, I owe him gratitude—for not putting me in jail when I got behind on child support and for not taking my children from me when I was drowning.

They say we have different compartments in our minds, and personalities that emerge in different seasons to protect who we are. All I know is that I was in survival mode, fighting or fleeing at all costs. I did what I did solely for money, to make ends meet, and the thick skin that grew morphed into a new roller derby persona—Muhammad Holly.

I remember the day my best friend called me, saying, "Come into town. I just bought skates at the shop in the Heights—we're going to play roller derby!" She had grand ideas, and I was the ride-or-die who made them happen. While roller derby was fleeting for her, it became my passion.

I dove in headfirst. Some skaters embody the term "roller derby saved my life," and for me, it did.

Let me be clear: Jesus saved my soul when I was a sophomore in high school, but roller derby saved me from the life I'd created for myself. It pulled me from a miserable pit I'd been in for three solid years. After that first practice, I sought more leagues and skating opportunities. I started "going straight," if you will. A good friend offered me a part-time job as a legal secretary in his personal injury law office and even though it began my use of cocaine in lieu of coffee, I was all too happy to type his dictation, redecorate his office, and get his afternoon "pick me up." In return, I made a modest living, had an alibi, and could leave work in time for derby practice.

My short-term cocaine use came to an abrupt end —I didn't play roller derby as well if I'd been snorting coke on coffee breaks. I started making healthier choices, attending more of my children's school functions, and became proud of my new job and a hobby that grew my confidence, released aggression, made me physically fit, and restored my sense of self. Soon

I had to find a more stable job, something "legitimately legitimate."

That's when the revolving door started again. No job feels right when a person isn't living God's purpose for them. It might seem like they "can't hold down a job," or they're flaky. Neither was true—I did well at every job I took, but each one felt like a poor fit. In an interview, one manager even told me, "You'll be bored here and end up quitting—but you can work here until you do."

And that's how it went. One job after another. Legal secretary, marketing specialist, administrative assistant, customer service representative, and technical writer. The final stop on this revolving door might have been my favorite. Someone took a chance on me as a quality control specialist at a metal repair shop. I worked fifty-one hours a week, with overtime pay after forty. (I was still playing roller derby at the team level, even on a travel team.) I thrived. My attention to detail was tested to the maximum, and the projects were endless. I led meetings on standard operating procedures every other week in front of fifty or more employees. As a bonus, I got to wear steel-toe boots and jeans to work every day.

But just like all the other jobs, I burned out and quit.

My messy life was a product created by desperation and weakness until the day my mother said, "Why don't you go back to school."

The thought of going back to school was a breath of fresh air. I knew if I ever had the chance, I would return and become an occupational therapist. After my eldest daughter's diagnosis of Highly Functioning Autism in 1999, I worked with her every day to bring her "up to speed" with the other children (whatever that means). We attended therapy at Texas Children's Hospital twice weekly back then, and in that, I grew a passion for working with children and helping them heal past the cards life had dealt. I would finally get the chance to have some purpose in life.

When I decided to take my mom up on the offer, I truly believed it would only take me four—five years max to get my master's—which was the requirement at that time to become an occupational therapist. I completed my associate's degree by attending class in the morning, coming home, taking a nap, and waking to study until two a.m.

I had the complete support of my children. My college-age son would take me for late-night energy drinks and Taco Bell runs, and I remember him saying, "No matter what, Mom, I will be at your graduation."

Then life happens, doesn't it?

The struggle was real, but at my age, grants and scholarships got me through my associate's degree completion. Once I reached the university level, I juggled working for the Dean of Students and working for a winery on weekends. I was within a year of completing my bachelor of science in fitness and human performance when my fourteen-year-old daughter cried for help in a way that would shake us to our core. My dreams were put on hold, and I dropped everything to support her as best I could, but that is her story to tell.

In the midst of all the tumult, God sent me a lifeline.

I met Marc while swiping right and left waiting for the next Uber fare. I took up driving for Uber as a way to make money and kill the long hours while my daughter was in treatment. I remember him walking into the Volcano Room that night.

And while I was only "casually dating" filling the small void for connection for a soul-mate, I thought to myself, *This could be the man I'm going to marry—this may be my last first date.* His baseball cap bobbed up and down, his face twitched with nervousness (and magnesium deficiency), as he talked of how he worked in chemistry and physics research—and I was hooked. Our date was short as I only had two hours to kill before picking up my daughter—a fact Marc still questions to this day (he maintains I left him that night for a second date). As I got into my car, my first call was to my best friend, "I think I'm going to marry the guy with Tourette's."

I was able to return to school the very next semester. Marc was very understanding of my schedule and agreed to Wednesday night sushi dates and weekends of watching football while I studied in his guest bedroom. With two final courses to complete in the mini-session, the opportunity of a lifetime presented itself. A course in gross anatomy opened up for undergraduates in association with Texas Chiropractic College. There, I met Dr. Robert Routh, PhD, who said to me, "You are selling yourself short—you need to become a doctor.

I believed my path was to become an occupational therapist; I was going to work at the Shriner's Hospital in the burn unit and was driven to get there.

And then Dr. Routh presented a fork in the road.

I began shadowing chiropractors and realized I needed more control over my patient's health—from "womb to tomb," they call it, and *that* was what I wanted. I wanted to make a difference in birth outcomes, to change the course of the life of a vaccine-injured infant, to catch scoliosis at a young age, to help my teen athletes have better games, to help women and men conceive, to give hope to women struggling through menopause and men through prostate issues, to provide life to years and years to life...to become a chiropractor.

The curriculum of a chiropractor is grueling, to say the least, but I ended trimester one with a 3.41 GPA. Completing ten trimesters, with twenty-one to twenty-six hours per trimester, year-round was daunting. During my first trimester of chiropractic school, I was met with appendicitis at midterms, the death of my beloved great aunt that Christmas, and then marriage to my sweet, supportive husband.

So, Marc and I lived happily ever after? Yes, but...

As with anyone who has a deep, dark secret, you hope those you love never find out, or that they'll forgive you if and when they do. I felt so bad on our wedding day about keeping it from him. I almost went to his groom's room just down the hallway to tell him before the wedding, but I took a huge chance that this was in my past and he wouldn't find out. After forty-three years of struggle, I had FINALLY found my soulmate and I didn't want the fairytale to end yet...and he didn't find out until two years later after we'd had our daughter.

I had just finished the Bible study *Breaking Free* by Beth Moore. I thought all I needed was for me to break free from my past's bondage, yet I was terrified he'd find out. One day, when our daughter was napping, I went into our bedroom and told him in tears, "I have something to tell you. You may hate me; you may divorce me. But I have to tell you, and I'm sorry I didn't tell you before we married."

His response?

"That was your past, and it's not who you are now."

Despite all my wrongs, God gave me the most understanding, gentle, kind, respectful, and loving man, created just for me, willing to love me past every flaw.

I'm convinced that God put me through illness and challenges throughout my life so that I could treat patients from a more empathetic perspective. After an amazing first trimester, I had to drop all of my second-trimester classes due to severe migraine headaches and fatigue which grounded me daily to the couch in the fetal position. My symptoms were presenting like Multiple Sclerosis and I saw medical doctors one after the other until I saw a neurologist who told me to take some vitamin B2 and come back in three months. Three *months*? I had about eight weeks before the next round of classes started and I needed help fast. That was when I encountered Esias Bacca DC.

He was a well-sought-after chiropractor who healed me through functional nutrition. He put me on an auto-immune protocol diet, fifteen minutes of push-pull weight training and fifteen minutes of cardio daily, and supplements catered to my lab work. Within six weeks I had shed twenty pounds of inflammation and was ready to return to chiropractic school.

Something happens when you get healthy—my peri-menopausal hormones returned to normal and at forty-five years old, I found out I was pregnant. This was a HUGE blessing to my sweet husband who thought God wanted him to "just be a dog dad."

On graduation day, I walked across the stage in nude heels, a tea-length navy dress with three-quarter sleeves, a pearl necklace, and matching earrings. My hair, razor-sharp in a pixie cut, was a testament to the confidence I now wore like armor.

"Holly Brocato," the Chief of Staff announced. With my mother and my daughters there as witnesses, two doctors draped a sash over my shoulders.

"Doctor Holly Brocato," the Chief announced again. Tears of pride rolled down my face, each drop cutting across a jaw worn sharp by years of choices—of blows and bruises only life's most challenging paths could sculpt.

I made a leap that my younger self would not have thought possible and I opened my own practice.

It took some doing, but eventually, we found the most perfect place in downtown Taylor, Texas. A place where I was in charge of the patients "from womb to tomb," could recommend nutritive supplementation, utilize my acupuncture training, prescribe therapeutic exercises, and spend more than seven minutes with my patients.

And so was born the Brocato Wellness Center.

The ribbon cutting was one of the most attended the Taylor Chamber of Commerce had ever seen. Patients came in droves to support God's plan of bringing health and wellness to the community.

Now if you live in Taylor, Texas or the surrounding area, you can see God's redemption story come to life.

We are all a living testament that God is a good God; redemption can be found.

DR. HOLLY NOEL BROCATO

Dr. Holly Noel Brocato is a distinguished chiropractor and owner of Brocato Wellness Center in Taylor, Texas. She holds a Doctorate in Chiropractic from Texas Chiropractic College and a Bachelor of Science in Human Biology, building on her earlier degree in Fitness and Human Performance from the University of Houston – Clear Lake.

Certified in the Webster Technique by the International Chiropractic Pediatric Association, Dr. Brocato specializes in perinatal and pediatric care. She's also trained in acupuncture and is pursuing certification from the Academy Council of Chiropractic Pediatrics.

As a keynote speaker, she advocates for holistic wellness through chiropractic, nutrition, and acupuncture principles. Dr. Brocato serves on the Taylor Chamber of Commerce and Taylor

Area Businesswomen while being an active member of First Baptist Church – Holland.

Website: brocatowellness.com
Facebook: facebook.com/profile.php?id=61563315892928
Instagram: @brocatowellness
LinkedIn: linkedin.com/in/dr-holly-brocato-dc-87b3bbb3

4

PRETTY DRUNK

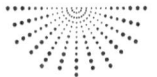

ALICIA RAFFKIND

I always thought I had it together. I always thought I had it under control —until I didn't.

The glass felt cool in my hand, but it was a distant comfort. Each gulp of wine hit the back of my throat hard, burning just enough to remind me that I was still here, still trying to keep it all together. The familiar haze descended. I wasn't sipping; I was devouring alcohol. I needed it—not to savor, but to quiet the gnawing inside me. The moon hung outside my window, indifferent to my nightly ritual. I stared at it, half hoping it might tell me when this would all stop. Would it ever stop?

I wiped my cheeks, swollen and damp with tears, knowing full well they would fall again tomorrow. There was always another tomorrow, another drink. My reflection in the bathroom mirror was a stranger. Lipstick was expertly applied, and the foundation was heavy enough to cover the tiredness creeping into my eyes. The white eyeliner was supposed to make me look awake, alive. But I knew. Under the makeup, under the clothes—designer heels, the immaculate dresses—I was barely holding on. No one saw that I was a "pretty drunk." Or so I thought.

At galas, weddings, and dinner parties, I played the role. Glass in hand, laughter in my throat, always "four drinks in" before anyone could suspect a thing. No one knew the frantic thoughts behind the facade. Would they notice if I slipped away to refill? Was there enough to last me the night? My routine was flawless, but it was also cracking. I couldn't hide forever, not even from myself.

I couldn't decide if I needed to negotiate with my struggles or surrender and get help. My health was rapidly declining, and I ignored all the alarm bells. Diagnosed with pancreatitis, I was so sick I could barely walk. I passed out in cars on the side of the road, woke up with bruises on my body, and blacked out night after night. My sleep patterns were insane—chugging booze to pass out and go back to sleep. I was barely eating, and when I did, it was crap. I was losing everything to alcohol, and it was depressing as hell. How did I let my life become about always getting high? I was living in a mega delusion.

Deep down, I knew a better life was possible and that sobriety was part of my plan. I always knew where I needed to be, but climbing out of the pit I dug for myself felt impossible. My brain was soaked in booze and I couldn't remember half of what I did. Every day was a mental battle— where was my next drink coming from? How would I survive another social event without making a fool of myself?

At those fancy parties, I had a system. If I ever tripped or stumbled, I'd "stop, drop, and roll" like nothing had happened, pick myself up, and carry on. But there came a point when I wasn't fooling anyone, not even myself. I wasn't just a "pretty drunk" anymore—I was habitually drunk. The push and pull of each day terrified me. And the truth was, I was scared out of my mind.

The days bled into each other, marked only by the question of when I could have my next drink. Vodka in the morning to jumpstart the day. Wine in my purse, hidden in the plastic bottles that wouldn't betray me with their clink. I'd look like I was living the dream - chardonnay in hand at ladies' night, vodka at the ready when I ran through the drive-up liquor store. The cashier knew me by name, and I wore it like a badge, masking the fact that I was losing control, losing everything.

You don't have to be homeless, broke, or jobless to be a drunk. You can look like a million bucks and still be spiraling. I was wasting my life, damaging my health, and yet I kept chugging because, in my mind, I still looked good. But even makeup couldn't hide the puffy eyes and swollen cheeks. My reflection wasn't pretty anymore. The dark blush I wore to hide my swollen cheeks made me look bruised. The exhaustion was consuming me.

And it wasn't just the physical piece that started to wear on me. I was doing absolutely nothing with my life. What did I stand for? What was my purpose? I was scared, knowing I was on a fast path to destruction and needed a way out. But quitting drinking felt impossible.

I became extremely afraid of what my next move was going to be to dig me out of this hell of alcoholism. Do I taper off, quit cold turkey, or manage my consumption? All these very dangerous ways of quitting drinking could be fatal. Tapering off was of no use, and managing consumption was a joke. When I tried quitting cold turkey, all hell broke loose and left me with hallucinating dreams, with me flying high in my bedroom and feeling like 100-foot mirrors surrounded me.

As time passed, I felt like a bottle of champagne exploding, bubbles everywhere, and I couldn't put them back in the bottle.

Then, one night, I knew something was off. I hadn't felt right—my stomach was churning, and my mind was foggy. I was lying down when suddenly I sat straight up, knowing I had to tell my husband, George. I forced myself down the stairs, but my legs felt like jelly. Each step was a struggle, my knees trembling under me. When I reached George, I crawled into bed beside him.

But the unease wouldn't let go. I sat up again, turning to him. "I feel really weird," I whispered, my voice shaky.

His eyes widened with concern. "Are you okay?" he asked.

I shook my head. "No. Not at all."

"Do I need to call 911?" he asked, reaching for the phone.

I could barely get the word out—"Yes"—before the seizure hit. My body went rigid, saliva foaming at my mouth, and my jaw clenched tight as I bit down hard on my tongue. George watched in horror, panic rising as he spoke to the 911 operator. Everything was happening so fast, and I was powerless, lying there motionless.

The Fire Department was the first to arrive. One of the men leaned over me, his voice cutting through the haze. "What's your name? Your date of birth?" My mind scrambled for clarity, but somehow I answered. Before long, the ambulance pulled up, and they whisked me away. On the ride to the hospital, I seized again, though I don't remember much of it.

Later, in the hospital room, a neurologist stood over me. "Are you diabetic or do you drink heavily?" he asked. I could only admit the truth— I drank heavily. They ran a series of tests, and I spent the night under observation.

You'd think the chaos would have changed me. But what was the first thing on my mind when I got home? I needed a drink. Even after all the mayhem, my brain still reached for the bottle. How twisted was that?

I was training for a half marathon back then, thinking I had things under control. One scorching afternoon, I decided to go for a run— but not before downing some vodka. I told myself that it was supposed to be a little boost. But instead, I ended up face down in a ditch, passed out. A friend found me, thank God, and called an ambulance. I can only imagine the shock and horror my husband must have felt, learning that his wife was sprawled out in a ditch, drunk and needing medical attention. I was a complete disaster, a hot mess.

You'd think that would have been a wake-up call. But no. When the actual race day came around, I repeated the same thing—chugging vodka before the run to keep myself from getting sick. It was a mess, and I was a mess, but I couldn't see how far I had fallen at the time.

Christmas was another rock bottom. I spent the whole holiday drinking, sneaking vodka or wine into my coffee cup while trying to act normal.

The truth was, I was anything but. I was nasty to my husband, taking all my anger and frustration out on him. He had finally had enough. After years of trying to cover for me, he told his family he couldn't keep doing it. That stung, but I was too deep in my addiction to care.

Then there was the trip—the one where everything unraveled even more. I woke up in the middle of the night, desperate for a drink, and grabbed a bottle of vodka. In my haze, I dropped it, shattering the glass all over the floor. I stepped right into the broken pieces, bleeding all over my feet, but I didn't stop. I just kept drinking, even as my husband begged me to put the bottle down. I was entirely out of my mind, lost to the addiction that had consumed me.

My organs were screaming at me to quit drinking. My liver, pancreas, and kidneys were shouting through my body, "Stop, for the love of God. We can't take this anymore. We're done, finished. We can't keep you alive."

Everything was shutting down at an alarming speed. My life was spiraling toward an end. My urine was dark like tea, vomiting was becoming more frequent, and my mind was spinning, completely lost, because I didn't know how to stop.

I had moved past "wanting" a drink—my body now "needed" it. Pouring a room-temperature glass of wine in the morning wasn't uncommon. I didn't have the luxury of waiting if there wasn't a chilled bottle in the fridge. A small gulp in the morning was enough to keep the shakes at bay. Without it, I felt horrible in a way that was impossible to describe. Every day, I was locked in this routine, my body aching and my stomach feeling like it was filled with acid. I couldn't muster the energy to drag myself out of my crumpled bed or even get dressed.

Was this the moment to shout, to scream from the mountaintops, "I have to quit"? I wanted to yell, "I want to live! I want to live! I want to live!" My husband had already told my father and brother-in-law, "I can't do this with her anymore."

This was the lowest point in my life. I didn't start my weekends until three thirty in the afternoon, and the first thing I reached for was chardonnay. No water, just wine—the tart, buttery taste of chardonnay was all that seemed to matter. I hadn't learned anything from Christmas or the nightmare at the beach. In my mind, all the rules were gone, and it felt like I was diving into an ocean filled with sharks. I was dodging a bullet with every drink, and alcohol poisoning was always lurking in the back of my mind, especially on vacations.

After Christmas and the disastrous beach trip, I scheduled an appointment with my doctor. I knew what the lab work would reveal—the truth I could no longer deny. I couldn't keep lying to her about "tapering off" or "cutting back." It was all a delusion, and I hated myself for needing to be there. My face was pale and swollen, and I looked terrible. Sitting on that table, waiting for the doctor, I was terrified. I knew I was on the verge of a stroke. I knew, I knew, I knew...

This visit was a turning point; either I was going to live, or I was going to die. My body was frail, bruised, and breaking.

The doctor walked in and immediately took my blood pressure, which was sky-high. She told me to calm down and then, with a stern voice, said, "Your labs don't lie. You're killing yourself." She gave me five to seven months to live at the rate I was going. She gave me two options: in-home treatment or a treatment facility. But I knew if I stayed home, I would head straight for another drink.

So I had to ask myself how many rock bottoms can one person have before they break? It seemed like I was mentally unstable, and I knew an intervention was inevitable. After years of shame, self-destruction, and praying for the strength to stop, I finally reached a point where I wanted to live again. I was desperate to stop getting drunk everyday and tired of being a disaster of a wife to my husband.

A treatment facility was my last hope. I was scared out of my mind, but I was ready. On February 28, 2014, my life changed forever. When I entered the center, I was so nervous. No cell phones, no TV, limited contact with the outside world. Counselors even separated my husband and me to ask tough questions about my success after treatment. When my husband came out of his room, he was crying. I told him not to worry—I was going to get better, I promised. He looked at me and said, "I'm not crying because of that. I know you'll get better. I'm crying because I just learned how much this place will cost!" We both laughed—a much-needed moment of comic relief.

I knew heading into detox for the next seven days would be brutal. Honestly, I thought I was going to die. At forty-two, I was staring down a life of sobriety, and it terrified me. Detox was pure hell —pounding headaches, vomiting for days, and when I did manage to sleep, it felt like I'd been in a coma for months. I barely left my room, too weak to move much, only stepping out a little at a time.

But something shifted. Even though my body was wrecked, I started eating healthier for the first time in years, small steps toward healing.

Rehab wasn't any easier—classes and counseling started at eight a.m. sharp and didn't let up for forty-five long, sober nights. But it was in those endless sessions that I began to talk about the exhaustion of being an alcoholic. Keeping the high was a full-time job. My tolerance was through the roof, and it drained me every single day. I had to keep track of my stash constantly— where were my little bottles of wine, the vodka hidden away? Did I have enough to get through? Reliving all that in my head made it painfully real again. Those memories hurt my spirit. I'd blown through cases of wine, and my whole existence had become about one thing: drinking and crashing.

It killed me to admit it, but I had pushed my faith away long ago. I thought God must've been tired of hearing me beg. "I'll cut back, I swear. I'll taper off. I promise this is the last time." Over and over, I prayed and pleaded, knowing it was a lie. I grew up in a Christian home, knowing right from wrong, but none of that mattered when I couldn't put the bottle down. That truth broke me.

In rehab, I cried—a lot. I had these wild, unsettling dreams where it felt like someone was always touching my head and hands. My addiction, like so many others, had its own twisted story, and somehow, those dark memories helped me survive the toughest nights. Each nightmare, each broken moment, became a piece of the battle I was finally facing head-on.

Nights were the scariest. I just wanted to fall asleep quickly to wake up the following day and keep going. I called it "sleep fast."

As my day to leave treatment drew near, I felt scared and fragile. I was anxious to get home, but I knew my biggest challenge would be overcoming the cravings for alcohol and staying sober. My husband was my rock, and I wanted to be a better wife and more compassionate toward him. I didn't want my life to always be about me and my appearance. I wanted to be more involved in the community and give back to those who cared for me.

I knew my faith and relationships with my family —whom I had been so isolated from—would never be unshakable again. But I was determined to rebuild them. My wisdom to speak up for what I believed in and let the light shine back into my eyes was returning. Nothing would steal my peace anymore, and I wouldn't be afraid of starting a career, even this late in life.

The pieces of my despair and darkness were turning into self-empowerment and self-love, and I was now in charge of negotiating my life to greatness. I was ready to step back, reflect, repolish, exhale, and love myself again, flaws and all. I was ready to become important again to the people I had left behind, to be hugged again.

I also decided to become involved with a nonprofit organization and strive to be a great volunteer. I found Downtown Women's Center through my husband's aunt, and I knew it would be a genuine fit. DWC specializes in helping women in Amarillo and the tri-state area who are struggling with addiction to drugs and alcohol. This reputable nonprofit organization touched my heartstrings because I understood these women. I could completely relate to their stories and their rock bottoms. It has helped me so much as a volunteer and mentor, giving me a sense of purpose in staying sober.

Many of my life experiences, both as an alcoholic and now as a sober person, have helped me become a recovery advocate. I've found pieces of my purpose. I'm not without struggles, but those difficult days are farther apart the longer I remain sober.

Volunteering with Downtown Women's Center for almost eleven years brought many perspectives into my life. I genuinely believe that these ladies were put into my life just as much as I was put into theirs. I always wanted to share my own story of alcoholism with them, but it was never about me—it was always about them. Listening to their stories of recovery, helping them however I could, hugging them, loving them, and seeing the light come back into their eyes—that's what mattered. I was humbled and honored to be part of the Downtown Women's

Center forever and I got to expand my message through speaking and writing.

Alcohol and drug addiction affect all walks of life. Nobody can tell who's in recovery just by looking at them. I know I'll be in recovery for the rest of my life. I've accepted these ten years of sobriety with all the greatness it has brought me, and my journey continues. Hope is always attainable. It comes with challenges, but it also brings exhilaration. With deep honesty, I can say, "I did it."

Sobriety is my daily choice, my battle, my victory. If my story has helped even one person, I know I've done my job by sharing it. And as I always say, *Keep on keeping on...*

ALICIA RAFFKIND

Alicia Raffkind is a community leader and advocate in Amarillo, Texas, recognized by the Amarillo Globe News as a "Citizen on the Move" in 2022. For over two decades, she has dedicated herself to transforming lives through her work with the Downtown Women's Center (DWC), serving two terms as board President and helping raise millions of dollars for women seeking recovery from addiction.

Drawing from her own decade-long sobriety journey, Alicia combines her passion for fashion with her commitment to helping others through the DWC's Dress for Success program. As President of the DWC Ladies Auxiliary and a volunteer at the Uptown Shoppe, she empowers women to rebuild their lives with dignity and style.

Alicia serves on the Amarillo College Foundation Board and regularly speaks about recovery, hope, and personal transformation. Her mantra, "Keep on Keeping on," reflects her unwavering dedication to supporting women on their path to recovery and self-discovery.

Linkedin: linkedin.com/in/alicia-walls-raffkind-10482b335
Instagram: @wallsraffkind
Facebook: https://www.facebook.com/alicia.walls.33/

5

THE DAY SHE TOOK BACK HER POWER

THERESA PORE

*T*he day began with the usual sense of anticipation—or should I say anxiety—that seemed to define most mornings. So much to do, the mental checklist ticking away in my mind. Bed made, check. Bible study and prayer time, check, check. My husband and I, as usual, argued over who had to get to work early and who would start our daughter's homeschooling for the day. Check, check, check. I almost always won that argument—he didn't want to touch seventh-grade literature. Finally, I sat down with my not-so-hot coffee and put on my mask. I mean, my makeup.

My vanity was cluttered with everything: seventeen shades of lipstick, eyeshadows for every season of the last two years, and five tubes of mascara—for fanning out, waterproofing, extending. Whatever it took to make the next Facebook Live that might sell one more tube of mascara. The beautifully restored makeup stand was like my life. Built to last, designed for beauty, joy, and hope for the future, yet tainted with overwhelm, clutter, and smudges.

I glanced at the mirror, not to see my reflection, but to check on the goals I'd clung to for five years—since I left my banking career to chase my dreams. Two phrases in red lipstick: "PINK Cadillac" and "Becoming the best." Achieving those would mean reaching the summit of success, finally making all the hard work worthwhile. I just needed the right strategy. Someday, it would happen. There had to be a way to get it done without compromising the parts of my life that demanded my attention.

Pushing aside the morning's chaos, I focused on the daily practice Coach Jo had taught me—visualization. I closed my eyes and saw myself on stage. A stage that welcomed my words. A stage built for dreams, inspiration, and hope for thousands of people. A stage I'd dreamt of for as long as I could remember, even before I became a sales director. I could see myself pouring life into the men and women in the audience. I imagined scales falling from their eyes, their ears opening, and a glow radiating from their hearts as God used my words to awaken their souls. Tears flowed as belief barriers shattered. Joy filled the room, and peace settled over me.

Then, like a thief in the night, that all-too-familiar voice crept in, hijacking my vision with a single soul-piercing question: "But Theresa, what if they find out?"

Ugh! Not again. When would this voice ever leave me? Every time I felt close to success, I could see myself in that space—no matter the platform, whether it was beauty, skincare, networking, or politics—this ugly reminder would emerge, pushing me back into mediocrity. At least, if I stayed small, no one would dig deeper or uncover the person behind the mask and the secret I had been carrying.

Frustrated, I cried out to God. "When?" I screamed, not holding back. "When will this ever end?"

I immediately felt a response deep in my spirit: "If you don't want them to find out, you tell them."

"Excuse me?" I shot back. "What's that supposed to mean?" I had carried this secret for twenty-seven years. How and why would I possibly expose myself and him to the consequences? Absolutely not.

A quote from Abby Johnson surfaced in my mind: "The enemy can no longer haunt you in the dark with what you expose to the light."

Haunting. Yes, that is the word to describe what I continued to experience. These subconscious taunts weren't the only way my past haunted me. It seeped into every relationship. I kept people at arm's length, never letting anyone get too close. Vulnerability felt dangerous. My emotions, once a compass, now felt foreign and unreliable. Shame clouded my thoughts, making me question my feelings, and so I shut down emotionally. This barrier didn't just keep friends and family at a distance—it crept into my marriage. The intimacy and connection I longed for were constantly blocked by guilt and the belief that my sexual desires were unclean.

The Holy Spirit pressed further, a relentless nudge in my soul: "Would you hold your thirteen-year-old daughter hostage to something that happened to her at that age?"

"No, of course not," I replied.

"Then why are you doing it to yourself?"

Hostage. Another loaded word.

My mind wandered as I considered what it meant to be a hostage—bound, fearful, helpless...

Yes. Every description hit home. The realization sank in. I had been holding myself hostage.

Maybe it was the last ten months of coaching, or perhaps it was just divine timing, but for some reason, my morning checklist was about to take an unexpected turn.

SHINING MY LIGHT

Excited to be in our new house, I jumped on my pink floral comforter, which complemented the pastel pink paint in my first big-girl bedroom. This full-size bed was a massive upgrade from the foam-green bunk beds my brother and I had shared in the "old house." Now, I had the bigger of the two rooms, with a view of the backyard and double mirrored closet doors. Princess Theresa had arrived!

I had my own space for the first time, not shared with my brother, sister, or countless cousins. This was what home felt like, which was new and different for me.

From birth, my life had been a little out of the ordinary. My parents had separated several times before I was even born—then they divorced. My dad moved to Texas, and shortly after, my brother and sister followed while I stayed with my mom, going from home to home with aunts, uncles, and cousins. Around eighteen months old, my dad received a call; "Your daughter is cute, but we can't keep her anymore. Can you pick her up?" This brought me to Texas, where I met my dad and my new mom—so many changes.

After countless nights of my sister's panic attacks and separation anxiety, she was sent back to live with our mom, and our family shifted once again. But now, Dad and Mom were happy, and I had the room closest to the bathroom. Life was grand with new friends, a new school, a new haircut, and a new family.

My parents weren't particularly religious, but my dad made sure I had reminders of God in my room. One of my favorites was a figurine of an open Bible, revealing the Lord's Prayer. I often caught him reading the Bible that sat on the dining room table. Seeds of faith were planted in me from a young age.

Moving to Leander, Texas, meant my parents' work routes had to change, as they now commuted to Austin from this isolated suburb. They needed to find a daycare to pick up me and Jason from school and take care of us during summers until we were old enough to walk home. Hill Top Baptist Church, right off HWY 183, was the best solution, allowing easy drop-offs and pick-ups.

Like any good church, the leaders quickly learned we didn't have a church foundation at home, so they arranged with my parents to scoop us up on the weekly church bus route. We spent countless hours on that bus, in Sunday school, and at the "big church." Singing songs and learning about God gave me a solid understanding, from the lens of an eight-year-old, of how to live—and how not to live.

I remember sitting "criss-cross applesauce" on the school bus, making hand signs while we sang, "This little light of mine, _I'm gonna_ let it shine..." When we got to "don't let Satan shh it out," we made exaggerated expressions, and I imagined the light in me shining so bright for the world to see.

I learned about the two foundations upon which you could "build your house." I learned about God's great punishment for sin, like the flood that killed everyone or how He turned people to stone for looking back at their old lifestyle. This created a deep fear that kept me on the straight and narrow. I'm sure my parents liked it. I could hold no secrets and probably took the fun out of parenting since I "told on" myself whenever I thought of doing something wrong.

Each time we went to church, my mind stored the data behind the scenes, like an AI program tracking my every move.

FROM LIGHT TO DARK

Entering sixth grade was especially exciting in our house. Once again, we would be in a new school with new friends, but something bigger was coming. Halfway through that year, as I discovered who I was (now Terry, not Theresa), my dad informed us that my sister was moving in. My sister? I had almost forgotten about her. It had been years since I'd seen her face. She was several years older than me, and I was beyond excited to see her again.

When she arrived, I was greeted by her nervous smile and three black trash bags full of clothes and possessions—things that would now fill my room. It took a while for us to warm up to her. I had so many questions and things I wanted to learn about the other side of my family, the part I hadn't seen since I was a baby. Who were they? How did they act? And most importantly, did they ever ask about me?

I'm not sure when the rules changed, but somehow, my sister living with us opened up an opportunity that had never existed before: contact with my mom.

I remember the first time I heard her voice. Whenever the phone rang, my brother, sister, and I would race down the stairs, knocking each other over to see who was calling. My house phone was the only number I cared to have memorized; it was etched in my mind. I was always waiting for that special call, thinking it would be my crush, JJ. But this time, it wasn't JJ— it was Susan, my biological mom.

Answering the phone the way I'd been taught, I said, "Hello, this is Theresa."

There was a pause, what seemed like forever. Then she said, "It's Susan, your mom." Tears filled my eyes as I sat there, soaking in the moment. I had no idea how just hearing her voice would give me back a piece of me that had been missing—a hole in my heart that only she could fill.

That phone call wasn't the only door we would walk through. As my brother and I entered middle school, hormones were in full force. His testosterone and "ADHD" were constantly getting him into trouble. As a last resort, my dad sent Jason to live with Susan.

"Let her handle him," he said.

I'm not sure if it was my and my sister's nagging or if my parents felt they needed a summer to themselves, but when the school year ended, Elizabeth and I took the Greyhound bus from Austin to Wichita, Kansas, to join Jason. I had not been outside of Texas since a toddler and never with strangers. The bus ride was both thrilling and terrifying at the same time.

Meeting my mom was overwhelming. I had that strange mix of joy, excitement, and fear. Was this right? Was it okay to call two people Mom? Was I somehow dishonoring my mom, Kim, by calling Susan Mom?

Liz and I were shown our new room in the cool attic space when the suitcases were finally unloaded. It was one of those rooms you'd see in old A-frame houses, with light floral wallpaper on the walls. The room was barely big enough for twin beds. I'd always wanted a secret room, and this felt like the perfect little nook.

The introductions started all over again when the brothers arrived from the baseball game. Jason brought familiarity back into view, but why did he seem so different? He had only been here a few months, but everything about him felt off—his talking, his clothes, even the way he carried himself. As I settled in, cousins, aunts, uncles, step-brother, and half-brothers started to appear, and I was swept up in a whirlwind of emotion. I was grateful to have a room where I could hide.

Coming from a sheltered upbringing, everything here was new. My stepdad was a truck driver, and my sweet, soft-spoken mom was left to handle five teenagers on her own—all taller than her and seemed to take advantage of her at every opportunity. The disciplined life I was used to quickly dissolved into one with no boundaries, rules, or accountability. It didn't take long to understand what had "changed" my brother. There was a strange feeling here—an absence of the familiar sense of security I'd grown up with, maybe even a wickedness I had never experienced.

At first, I didn't notice how things were shifting. Maybe it was my naive and trusting heart, but soon, I was trapped. I remember the first time he hugged me. It was awkward, like something out of a movie. He had just returned from a baseball game—it was August and HOT. He smelled like a mixture of dirt, sweat, and sunflower seeds. When he bent down to hug me, he picked me up and spun me around. At thirteen, I was only 4'10" and about ninety pounds, no match for his six-foot, 180-pound frame. When my stepdad was gone, he took over as the authority in the house. Everyone did what he said. Before long, I was living a secret life I couldn't tell anyone about.

In the middle of the night, he would wake me up. I could count on it like clockwork. Once the sound of *I Love Lucy* turned off and Mom went to bed, I would be "invited" downstairs to the living room and told to do things I didn't understand. First experiences weren't supposed to be this way. I was supposed to be in love. Why was my body reacting in ways that contradicted my emotions and beliefs?

When I couldn't make sense of it, I went into autopilot, shutting down to avoid guilt and shame. Once foreign to me, control, manipulation, and secrecy became my reality. In twelve months, I had aged what felt like ten years. My little light seemed to have been blown out. Instead of shining, all I wanted to do was hide.

My dad and mom visited us once while we were in Kansas. They could tell something was wrong. The lack of sleep had taken a toll on me. My grades suffered, and I lost much of my kindness. I had always been the child who "spilled the beans," so they trusted that everything was okay, even though they must have known something was off. I, too, had changed. Like my brother, I looked dark, unhealthy, and different.

When the opportunity came to return home to my life of routine, structure, and expectations, I couldn't get there fast enough. Before leaving Kansas, I made myself a vow; I would never let anyone get "inside me" again. The vow of a thirteen-year-old should never be underestimated. We are, after all, made in God's image, with the power to speak things into life. I had no idea this declaration would construct a wall around my heart, body, and mind.

A NEW ROUTINE

Moving back with my dad seemed like an easy transition. While we were in Kansas, he and my mom moved to his hometown in Indiana to help his family with some health concerns. No one in this state knew me; even the family I would meet didn't know who I had been before Kansas. It felt like it would be easy to put that experience away —bury it in the past, never to be dealt with or thought about again. It was easy to hide the awkwardness. I could blame it on the new house, new school, new kids, new friends. It was easy to hide how my clothes had changed because everyone changed in high school, right?

However, how I interacted with other people wasn't so easy to hide. There was so much conflict inside me now. Questions constantly ran through my mind: Who could I trust? What was love? What was "appropriate" love? Which expressions of love were okay? What were the red flags?

My dad and mom didn't show us affection through physical touch. Hand-holding was rare, and hugs, when they happened, were short and distant. We felt love, no doubt, but it wasn't expressed physically. In Kansas, the pendulum swung the other way—touch had no boundaries, and that confusion followed me. Any expression of love became challenging. I always felt awkward, unsure if I might allow someone to manipulate me again.

My solution was to control the outcome by not letting people in when they got too close. With each relationship, I would start off trusting, allowing room for love to form, but I'd quickly set up mental and emotional blocks. This became the pattern of my life and how I processed friendships and relationships with boyfriends. It was the programming I carried into my marriage and let flow into my career.

Unfortunately, the more I built up that resistance to people, the more my ability to trust diminished. It made reaching people on a level of empathy and impact incredibly difficult.

WHO IS IN CONTROL HERE, ANYWAY?

Mind control was always an ambiguous theory to me. I'd heard stories my entire life of "brainwashing" and puppet master techniques that suggested someone or something outside of us was controlling our circumstances—like the idea that at the click of a button, or if told something enough times, we'd be forced to believe it. But what I had come to realize was that mind control for most of us isn't external. The one in charge is internal—the program running the show, deeply buried in the subconscious mind.

My early years programmed me to believe that the decisions I made—or allowed to be made for me—would condemn me for life. The solution I developed during those identity-forming years was simple: hide who you are, stay out of the light, protect yourself from being taken advantage of, and you'll be safe. The problem was, like a virus running silently in the background of a computer, I didn't even know this program was running.

So, there I was, sitting in my bedroom at forty years old—frustrated, lost, and not living my #bestlife. I had two daughters, a bonus son, and a husband of twenty years who still adored me, even though I'd been pushing him away for a long time. I kept hitting roadblock after roadblock. I'd reach a certain level in my business, then—BAM—I'd hit a wall. I'd get comfortable enough to make friends, then—BAM —another barrier keeping them from getting too close. I even found myself feeling awkward about showing too much affection to my children. It was like a shield, protecting me—or maybe protecting them—I wasn't sure which. And now, God was telling me to expose my past to step into my future.

I quickly dismissed the argument going on in my spirit, refocusing so I could get on with my day. After all, it was September, which meant a new homeschool year to prepare for and gearing up for the busy winter season in our chimney business.

Reaching down to pick up the blow dryer, I rolled my eyes, discovering that the housekeeper had unplugged it again. As I bent over to plug back in, a spark ignited, reminding me of a glimmer of light..."This little light of mine." I wondered if it would ever shine again. Would I ever reach the place where I fulfilled my God-given purpose of sharing my light with the world?

LET IT SHINE

For several weeks, I had been building up my team, anticipating the fall retreat we were attending. It wasn't just any retreat—it was our first in-person event since March 2020, called "Celebrate the Harvest." I knew this could be the event that would change everything. After all, "Theresa" means "harvest."

Two friends from our Sister Director Circle and I were asked to provide a piece of hope and inspiration during the Sunday Sunrise service. We decided our topic would focus on individual gifts, talents, and purpose. Cynthia would speak about the uniqueness of each of us, Julie would cover individual strengths and spiritual gifts, and my role was to share what holds us back from stepping into purpose. I had three pages of notes, starting with Mark chapter four, filled with Theresa-isms, ready to go.

Waking up three hours earlier than intended, I slipped out to my car to pray, asking God for the right words and open eyes, ears, and hearts. I was ready to pour out my heart to these women, hoping to spark a fire that would help them pursue their goals.

Julie wrapped up her segment with grace and eloquence, and I knew it was my time. The usual mix of excitement, nausea, nerves, and imposter syndrome hit me simultaneously. Grabbing my notes and Bible, I took the mic. After a few moments of thanking Julie and Cynthia, the usual pleasantries, I jumped into my notes.

Somewhere along the first page, though, the Holy Spirit took over. I was supposed to discuss what keeps us from fulfilling our purpose, but all my notes became unnecessary. I found myself sharing "my truth"—what had held me back for so long. The secret that kept me at a distance from everyone.

Like a pig gutted at slaughter, I laid it all out. This truth, the meaning I'd given to this one event, had allowed me to become a victim trapped in an invisible cage. It wasn't a lack of talent, strategy, resources, or influence holding me back—it was my secret and the control it had over me. I had buried it for years out of fear: fear of feeling like a phony, fear of accusations or being judged, fear of being discovered, fear of God's wrath. This fear led to self-sabotage and, ultimately, a fear of success.

As I came to a close, the "oh crap" feeling kicked in. You know, the one you get when you accidentally say something way too big to take back? Like a camel coming through the eye of a needle, I had just released this giant secret that could never go back inside. I wasn't sure if I felt relief, humiliation, fear, or some combination of all three, but I was grateful for the years of impromptu speaking practice in high school because I was *so* far off-topic.

Or was I?

When I finished, the room was silent. You could've heard a pin drop. All I could think was, *Okay, God, I trusted you. I let you lead. Now what?*

To my amazement, no stones were thrown, no mocking comments—instead, a standing ovation. I saw faces streaked with tears and tissues falling to the ground. Looking at the audience, I saw what I had only ever seen in my dreams: an awakening. My story had done more than inspire hope or strategy to reach goals—they didn't need strategy any more than I did. They needed what I had just unlocked—freedom from the invisible emotional handcuffs they'd been trapped by. As I shared, it became clear that many of them had also been victims of shame, guilt, or fear, and something powerful happened in that room that morning.

Shame is a load we were never meant to carry. It crushes us when we keep it inside.

The light inside me—the one the enemy had tried to extinguish with shame, guilt, defeat, and darkness—was finally reignited.

Inside each of us, there is a light. We are hardwired with it. Some call it energy, and some call it purpose. I like to call it power. Like a computer infected with viruses, life's interruptions and struggles can drain us, pulling us from that power source and leaving us ineffective. However, when we step away from those distractions and look inward, we find that those interruptions and struggles are the pieces that lead us to purpose.

That day in October 2021 was indeed a celebration. It was the day I took back my power. And in doing so, I gave others permission to do the same.

This little light of mine... I'm gonna let it shine!

THERESA PORE

As a Keynote Speaker, Trainer, and Coach, Theresa Pore uses life lessons from two decades of marriage, sixteen years of work in the financial services industry, community leadership roles, developing and running business-to-business networking organizations, successfully navigating mergers and acquisitions, and owner operating several businesses to help men and women build resilience and create their success.

Theresa hosts the UnBreakable Women's Conference™, which focuses on helping women "take back their power" by turning broken pieces into purpose. Theresa and her husband, Royal, founded UnBreakable Enterprises LLC, which takes the elements of UnBreakable Life™ (self-discovery, mindset, personal beliefs, defining moments/ trauma, health, community, and purpose) and makes them universal to relationships, businesses, marriages, and families.

Theresa's Mission: "Helping you live your life's purpose by living your life on purpose."

Linkedin Theresa Theresa
Instagram theresapore320
YouTube @theresapore5980
Website theresapore.com
unbreakable-business.com

6

BETTER TO BE LUCKY, THAN TO BE GOOD...OR IS IT?

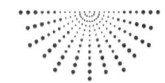

MELINDA GARVEY

Sometimes, it's only in hindsight that you understand how you arrived at this moment in life. Have you ever driven home, and only once you pull into the driveway do you realize you don't remember how you got there?

That's how I feel.

I've been driving for over forty years (I got my license in the womb), and while I've enjoyed the views and stopped in many places, here I am, sitting in the metaphorical driveway, wondering exactly how I got here.

So where is "here?"

Today, after twenty-two years, I'm stepping back from my day-to-day role at the company I founded, *Austin Woman* magazine. I'm also winding down the SaaS company I founded, *On The Dot*. And because "taking a break" isn't in my DNA, I'm launching a new venture: *InHer Circle*, a peer advisory group for women.

I was born lucky—into a family that loved me fiercely and believed I hung the moon. And they told me, over and over, that hanging that moon wasn't just a dream; it was within my power. We had means, though I wouldn't fully understand that until later. I got an excellent education without a penny of debt, and my parents were my role models for deep, lasting relationships, not just with each other but with lifelong friends they cherished and nurtured. I traveled the world and was exposed to many interests: theater, philanthropy, cooking, boating, reading, and perhaps most importantly, an interest in people— people like me, people who weren't, and people more and less fortunate.

Lately, I've been reflecting on my journey, not just on *where* I am in my life, career, and circumstances but on *who* I am and the forces that shaped me. Yes, I was lucky, but my journey wasn't all smooth sailing. Over time, I've realized that the challenges, failures, and heartbreaks may have had an even more significant impact on who I am today than the lucky breaks.

My beloved brother died of cancer at just twenty-six. He's been gone thirty-two years now, but sometimes the loss still takes my breath away. At the age of twenty-four, I learned that life is painfully short. People leave you, even when it's not by choice.

And so, I've always held on tight to my people. However, I'm still learning that others don't always hold on as tightly. And when I ease my grip or let go a little to see if they'll reach back, some do, and some don't. One of my friends often says, "Friendships have seasons," but I struggle to see it that way. I think daily about the friends I've lost and wonder if I'll ever stop feeling the ache— or if that's just how it is for me. On the other hand, I have friends who've been in my life for over forty years (yes, friends from the womb), and they still feel like home.

My brother's death didn't just leave an emotional mark—it also drove me to push myself harder and influenced so many of the pivotal choices I've made. I wonder if I would've had the courage to take the risks I did: starting three companies, riding the entrepreneurial roller coaster with all its dizzying ups and downs, and living life on my terms. There was also this sense of responsibility, this desire to be successful, even "good," as the only child left—as if I had to achieve for both of us. That pressure was entirely self-imposed, and looking back, I can smile at it, but I wouldn't change a thing. Sometimes, we have to make sense of tragedy in our own way, and if that experience drove me first to discover my passion, then pursue it, and finally succeed at it, then I'm grateful for that lesson. I know my brother would be proud.

So, how did I get to this point, sitting in my driveway wondering how I got here and where I'm going next?

I was ten years into my career—promotions, flying colors, and all—when I decided to move back to my hometown of Indianapolis to be near family after eleven years in Washington, D.C. A promising management role at a radio station (which shall remain nameless) awaited me. I had worked at an advertising agency for nearly four years right out of college, then moved on to a group of suburban daily newspapers. I eventually became the youngest VP of Sales and Marketing in a senior leadership position. But when I left

D.C. for Indianapolis, it was as if the universe decided to have some fun with me.

And boy, was I about to get an education.

It all started with a series of misogynistic, arrogant, and untrustworthy men. Now, before you go thinking I'm male-bashing, understand this: I grew up surrounded by positive, encouraging male role models. My dad, brother, early bosses, and mentors supported, promoted, and pushed me to do more. So, naturally, I thought I was landing a fantastic role with a great, respected company back in Indianapolis. As far as I knew, this girl was still riding the express elevator to the top. I didn't realize that I was indeed on a ride—more like the kind where you're at the top floor of a skyscraper, and suddenly, the elevator cables snap.

My boss turned out to be a washed-up DJ with gold chains and a penchant for making lewd and suggestive comments to women in the office—particularly the sales reps who worked for me. Apparently, if you wear gold chains, leave at least three shirt buttons undone, and go by a two-letter name from your DJ days, you can call out the "hot" young sales reps. Since I was the only female manager, I quickly had a line at my door of people complaining about him. I reported him, of course...and was promptly fired. Yes, you read that right. Even the over-fifty HR director from the parent company told me I should have kept my mouth shut.

You could've knocked me over with a feather.

Remember when I said it's "better to be lucky than good"? I'd been very lucky—I just didn't know it yet. Now, I was utterly unprepared to handle a situation like this. I wallowed in shame, in a newfound lack of confidence where once there had been plenty, and in disbelief.

So, I flew to Austin, Texas, to visit a friend and lick my wounds.

In Austin, I fell in love with the city at first sight. I immediately started looking for jobs, and within two weeks, I had a fantastic offer that included a free apartment for a year, great pay, and, best of all, I was the top dog in the office.

Or so I thought.

The senior sales rep (a woman) had applied for my job and didn't get it, so she was all too eager to derail and discredit me at every turn—something I'd never experienced in my charmed life. My boss lived in Houston but called every morning at 8:25 a.m. to ensure I was running the mandatory (and largely pointless) daily sales meeting. When I suggested we might not need this meeting daily, she clarified that I was to do as told.

And then the topper: the regional VP from Arizona decided to surprise us with a visit, and in the sales meeting, he announced, "I'm the head mother-fucker!"—just in case anyone needed reminding of who was in charge. I looked around the room, half-expecting everyone to burst into laughter and acknowledge this as some caveman's attempt at breaking the ice. But no, this was real. The looks of terror on my team's faces told me as much, and the fact that the self-proclaimed head mother-fucker didn't smile or slow his aggressive pacing up and down the conference room just added to the drama. So, this was the infamous "lead by intimidation" method. Huh.

After such a glorious and successful start, I began to spin out, wondering how I'd landed in this alternate universe. "Lucky" and "good" weren't cutting it this time. My confidence was gone; I questioned my every move, suffered daily migraines at work, and was generally a wreck.

So, out I went with my friend and a few of her friends to drink wine (as you do) and lament my job situation, trying to figure out what was next. But as women do so well, we ordered a bold cabernet and started brainstorming my next move.

Suddenly, my friend chimed in, "Hey! I just got back from Des Moines, Iowa!"

We all stared at her like she had three heads.

WTF? I thought. *This is my pity party, and you're talking about Des Moines, Iowa?*

But out loud, I said, "By all means, tell us about your trip."

She needed no further encouragement. "There's this magazine called *Des Moines Woman*," she said. "It tells stories of incredible, inspirational women—that's what *you* should do! You have a publishing background. And no one's doing this for women in Austin."

This was during Austin's first tech boom, and she was right—female changemakers weren't getting the spotlight. Goosebumps crept up my arms, and the hair on the back of my neck and, probably, my whole head stood up. I felt like I'd been struck by lightning. I knew, with utter certainty, this was my calling. *This* was why the universe put those back-to-back misogynistic roadblocks in my way and sent my career careening off a cliff. This was what I was meant to do.

With the support of that remarkable group of women (one of whom became my business partner), I started writing a business plan the following day. Two weeks later, I was "fired-quit" from my job working for "the head mother-fucker" and embarked on the journey of a lifetime. Seven months later, in September of 2002, we published the first issue of *Austin Woman*, with Amy Miller Simmons of Amy's Ice Cream on the cover.

Those early years with *Austin Woman* were surreal. We set out to give women a voice and tell their stories to inspire others, and we did it. The feedback was tremendous, and the magazine was an instant hit. We grew, added events, and did everything possible to fulfill our mission.

Then, in the blink of an eye, it was 2022, and *Austin Woman* had turned twenty. I wondered what the next twenty years would bring and thought maybe it was time to sell and "retire."

But then, it happened again. I told you I was lucky.

After a conference, I was chatting by the pool with two trusted, badass women about what might be next. "Should I just sell?" I asked them. I was proud of how we'd championed women and leaned into diversity, equity, and inclusion (even as DEI became a "dirty" word in 2024), and I wanted that legacy to continue.

Then it struck me.

"Why must the leader be one person? What if we created a consortium of diverse women to carry on this mission?"

My friends' jaws dropped.

One said, "Are you serious? Because if you are, I'm in!"

Then the other echoed, "Me too!"

And just like that, AW 2.0 was born.

Today, *Austin Woman* is owned by eight women, including myself—two African American women, two Latina women, one Asian Pacific Islander woman, one Indian woman, and two white women. I believe we made history that day.

The power of women coming together for a shared mission can make anything happen. And a margarita or two doesn't hurt!

Somewhere in the midst of all this, I launched a tech company called On The Dot.

Yes, a SaaS company.

I stumbled backward in heels into tech and developed a virtual community software platform. Strangely enough, it's one of the accomplishments of which I'm most proud.

Why?

Because I never imagined a fifty-year-old English Lit major could raise capital, build software, and manage a company with—if I do say so myself—a pretty damn good product. Had I stopped to think about it, I might never have done it. But the journey taught me something invaluable: sometimes, one step after another opens the doors to achievements of which you never knew you were capable.

So what now? *Austin Woman* is on a new path, and On The Dot has licensed its software and wound down daily operations. While stepping away from the frenetic pace of the last twenty years felt strange, I knew I needed a break from the chaos. The stress and pressure had often left me feeling unrecognizable to myself. It took time to let go, but once I did, something interesting happened—my mind opened to new possibilities. Most importantly, I found myself getting excited about solving another problem.

If I had a dollar for every person who told me I should be a "coach" while figuring out my next move, I could have retired by now. But while I agreed I'd be good at it—I'd built two companies, restructured and sold one, raised money to fund another, and picked up countless skills as an entrepreneur over twenty-two years—something was holding me back.

I like to dive deep, both in friendships and in business. I love learning what makes people and businesses tick. When I join a nonprofit board, for example, I go all in to understand its mission to be a passionate advocate. "Coaching" or "Advising" felt too surface. I know it doesn't have to be, but in my experience, that's often the case. Most coaches I've worked with were great at helping me manage my mental state related to business. But, none had the depth of understanding of my business to offer actionable advice, recognize opportunities, or guide me through a cash-flow crisis. You get my drift.

That's when I discovered something called Peer Advisory. It's a small group of business owners who meet monthly with a facilitator to discuss each other's businesses. The group uses its collective experience and insights to help each other overcome hurdles, grow, and scale. The problem? Most of these groups are very male-dominated—often just one or two women in a room full of men. And while I love men, let's face it: women do things differently.

Standing up and being heard is hard when you're the minority. So, I decided to change that with the launch of *InHer Circle: Peer Advisory for Women*.

InHer Circle brings eight female business owners together as each other's personal advisory board, plus what I call "coaching with context" with me. And I'm so excited about this I can hardly stand it. I love solving problems, and now I can help other women solve theirs. And when those "other people" are women who often face more challenges raising capital, finding mentors, and securing the connections they need to grow and scale—it's a no-brainer.

Purpose is at my core. I didn't always know that. Early in my career, I liked my jobs, but I wasn't searching for some higher purpose—I didn't even know I had one until it hit me between the eyes. And once you see it, there's no going back. Purpose isn't something you can unsee. I tried; I veered away from it when I founded a SaaS company, convinced that challenge alone would bring fulfillment. But it didn't. I'm proud of what I built in tech, but those seven years were the hardest of my life because I wasn't aligned with what truly drove me.

Now, I see that purpose isn't just about passion or success. It's about resilience, about learning to hold onto what matters through every lucky break and every heartbreaking setback. It's about embracing that mix of luck, failure, and skill, understanding that each plays its part but that growth lies in what we do with all of it. For me, purpose is about honoring my journey—and those I've lost along the way—by relentlessly pursuing what I believe in.

And in doing that, I'm finally right where I need to be.

MELINDA GARVEY

Melinda Garvey is a serial entrepreneur, founding her first company, *Austin Woman*, twenty-two years ago and then just recently executing a successful and unprecedented organizational restructure to bring on nine additional diverse female owners as partners.

"This new leadership structure allows us to realize the huge growth potential of *Austin Woman*, while at the same time ensuring the magazine continues its legacy of inclusion for generations to come." Garvey is also the founder of *On The Dot*, a B2B, SaaS Virtual Community Platform.

As Garvey winds down from her day-to-day operations role at *Austin Woman*, she is focused on her new company, *InHer Circle*, Peer Advisory for Women where she will facilitate and advise a small group of female business owners who are scaling to and beyond the million dollar mark.

Garvey is married to Kiwi husband, Kip, and together they have a seventeen-year-old son, Beck. When not with her boys or working, you will find her surrounded by inspiring women and drinking wine!

7

BUTTERFLIES FROM GOD

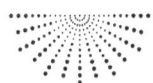

REBECCA ANNE PRICE

*I*n my dark, musty room, surrounded by hopelessness, anxiety pressed like a tire on my heart. Every breath was filled with thoughts of despair. Nobody ever wanted me and I had plenty of evidence to prove it. I pondered every word that was spoken over me.

"You are a failure."

"You stink! I would never be your friend."

"You will NEVER amount to anything. You might as well drop out of school," said my seventh-grade history teacher.

I was told by every adult and every peer in my life from birth that I was a mistake. I was told I had no value.

I sojourned throughout my life as a nomad. From the moment I woke up until I crashed on my pillow or some sort of bed at night, the thought that screamed loudest in my mind was that no one in the world cared about me. One day while I was watching the Discovery Channel, I saw a program about worms.

I felt like a worm. The song I used to sing was, "Nobody likes me, everybody hates me, I guess I'll go out and eat some worms. Yucky little green ones, gooey little red ones, I guess I'll go out and eat some worms."

When watching about worms, I was drawn into one story about a caterpillar that changes into a butterfly. I felt there was no way anyone could know how and what I was feeling or going through. Yet just maybe that caterpillar does. She goes through life ugly and seemingly wandering. The deep feeling of loneliness was confirmed. I saw how separate and insignificant the worm lived.

The smell of fear, death, and decay penetrated my nostrils as I began to ponder the end. Would anyone find me? Would they care? As darkness closed around my mind, I looked out the window.

The sun was shining through the curtain as dust floated in the room. I sat. Thinking. Waiting.

The sound of a car door slammed twice. The crushing sound of the car tires moving closer up the driveway and then the sudden stop and sound of the car honking caused a momentary break from the crushing feeling of despair.

I jumped to my feet and ran to open the door. I said to myself "Smile, they will never know." Mom shouted, "Hey babe, we will be back in an hour. We have a bowling event." Knowing my destiny was waiting for me in the garage, I waved. The emotions on the inside did not betray me. "See you then," I shouted, and waved like I was eager to see them again.

My heart raced as the car inched out of the driveway. Then, like a turning of the page, they were gone.

Finally, no one will know till I'm gone, no one will be around to stop me, I will never have to feel like I have failed the world any longer, went through my head. I ran to the garage with determination and a drive to finally be in control of my life, my choices, and what happens to me.

Yes, even if this was the wrong choice, it was mine to make. I hurt. It crippled my mind. There was the constant mental weight of disappointment. I could no longer take the failure, despair, hopelessness, disappointment, anger, and abandonment that had become the glaring birthmark of my life.

I stumbled through many years of junk piled in our musky garage. The space was full of memories, multiple moves, carelessness, and it looked like a garbage truck had picked up stinky, slimy trash from multiple homes and dumped it there. Buckets of black sludge. Piles of clothes that had been abandoned to rot in the heat. I looked around and was drawn into a deeper despair as I gazed at the disregarded possessions.

I related to the broken doll that sat in the corner. Why didn't anyone want her? What did she do wrong? She once was loved unconditionally and now she is discarded, alone, seeming to be tossed away into the pit of the forgotten.

I searched the garage from corner to corner. Turning. Throwing. Screaming. Desperate. "Where is it? Where is it? I know it is here. It must be here. I saw it. I know it's here." I began to hyperventilate. "WHERE IS IT?"

OH, WHERE IS IT? I wondered. *I need to find it. It's the only thing I have left. Oh, I can't even do THIS right.*

I truly am nothing...worthless, rang loudly through my head. I needed this to be the end. But how does one get here to think these thoughts? What kind of life could be so terrible that I'd prefer not to have one at all? Tracking back to the beginning is the only way to calculate the decision.

* * *

The doctor told my mother the tests were inconclusive. "She is one point shy of cystic fibrosis. The best you can do is take her home and love her for the days she has left.

We don't know how long. She will surely die," the doctor said.

My mother was wrought with utter emptiness as to what she was to do. She couldn't afford to pour into this child and just have it taken from her in death. We went home and went through the daily routine minus the bonding. There were days I lay in my baby bed and cried. There were days I was left alone to die.

My aunt and uncle (my mom's sister and brother) visited often and bonded with me. They gave me a sense of worth from their spurts of love and interaction. They were my saving grace. Their love helped me to thrive, to find a spark of life within my struggling little body. Over the years, the excitement when my aunt and uncle came was unmatched by anything. It was my hope and continued energy source.

I was third in line of four kids. Our lives were a constant battle to see who could control the day. We fought, we tore each other down, and had no respect for each other. What would be the expectation when that was the example set before us?

As I grew, I began to spend time by myself. I learned to imagine and pretend for a better life. I watched shows like: *Little House on the Prairie*, *The Hulk, Star Trek*, and Sunday Disney shows. These programs were where I found my morality. I wanted to be good. I wanted people to like me. When I watched these shows, I learned that if you give your best, you will be appreciated.

In third grade, I had the opportunity to put this to the test. A week before Christmas break, we were asked by our teacher to buy a gift to be exchanged in class the next week.

"Mom, I need a gift." I said. After she ignored me I persisted, "MOM, I need a gift!" Each time she walked away and ignored my request. Frustrated, I remembered the episode that said if you give your best, you will be appreciated. Then, I recalled when the character on *Little House on the Prairie* gave a gift, she gave her favorite ribbons because she had nothing else to offer. So, I hatched a plan.

That night, I sat up in my dark room. The smell of raw wood, dust, and rodent poop filled the air. Peering through the darkness, I searched for the box. Placing the box on my bed, hope and excitement poured over me. Maybe, just maybe, I could be normal. I longed to dress like the other girls. I was desperate to be welcomed and wanted by my community. The overwhelming need to be wanted pulsed through my veins. From kindergarten through third grade, there were debilitating circumstances that molded my place in society.

Daily, once or twice or three times a day, a terrible stench emanated from me, repelling the kids in the entire room. The teacher that was stuck with me had to deal with the disgusting chore of cleaning up the poopy pants accidents. I had no control over my bowels. My parents said this was from laziness (after I became an adult the doctors told me they believed it was a side effect of the cystic fibrosis diagnosis). I was labeled "stinky" by my peers and the teachers.

"Teacher, Beckie stinks again" came a shrill from the girl next to me. A feeling of great despair came over me.

Oh no, not again! My dad is going to beat me when I get home.

The rest of the day I was distracted with the anticipation of the coming physical beating.

Wretched with fear, I could think of nothing else. When I got home, I tried to find ways to hide. These efforts never worked. Dad came home at five p.m. and the first words out of his mouth were "Well?"

I tried to lie, which made it even worse because lying was a cardinal sin. So I would get beat with a leather belt that was rimmed with metal strips that he created just for this purpose.

Screaming like I was being crushed, I heard, "If you cry any more, I will continue to spank you." With his hand in my hair, holding me where he could beat me, I began to muster up the fortitude to stop crying. This was my journey of learning to hide my emotions and feelings and play the part. I thought if I would just look like everyone else on the outside, I would survive.

Christmas is a very special day when dreams come true. My hero, my hope, everything about Christmas made me well up with anticipation. This day is what makes dreams come true. I believed if I could just be good or if I could just get on the good list, this would be my chance to get out of this horrible life.

My teacher told me to bring a gift. She said we would exchange them on Monday and everyone who brings a gift will get a gift. The idea that I could have a moment of being a part of something comforted me, and I began to laugh and giggle wishing Monday would come quickly. I packaged my favorite doll that I had had since I was a baby. This doll was my everything. The squares on the corner of the wrapping had to be perfect (in full disclosure, the wrapping of this gift was less than desirable. You could so tell it was from a child).

The ribbon was beautiful, and it was ready for school. On Monday morning, I shot out of bed thinking today is my day—the day I will be liked! I rummaged through the pile of stinky clothes in my room and found an outfit that would make anyone proud. It was a cotton, cream-colored shirt with short ruffles on the front, running from the neckline down the middle. I was oblivious that the smell of old sweat and dirt permeated from my shirt and wafted down the hallway as I walked. I had no idea of my state; it was the smell of life to me.

I sat in my chair in utter excitement when the teacher said "Class it's time. Everyone can get a gift from under the tree." I ran and got what looked like a deck of cards. *What could it be? Oh, this is so exciting,* I thought. I ripped off the packaging to reveal a sewing kit. So cool! I always wanted to learn to sew. This was *mine.*

Suddenly a scream of utter disappointment rang through the classroom. As I turned to see where it came from, the teacher hovered over me. I felt a strong thrust of an object forced into my arms. Totally confused, the sewing kit was violently snatched from my hands. I was completely shocked and perplexed.

The teacher yelled at me and told me to go away. The child who received my most precious gift hated it. She screamed; the teacher came running only to find a wrinkled broken box. Inside the box there was a baby doll. The doll had hair that was so matted it looked like dog poop. The body of this doll was urine-stained and filthy. The arms had color marks with drawings pasted on them. The fingernails looked like they were painted 29 different times. This gift was not a gift but a joke.

That was what the teacher thought. "Beckie, this is a cruel joke. You should be ashamed," said my teacher in front of the other students.

My life was rattled with similar stories. One by one these stories built a wall. This wall was thicker and more dense than the Great Wall Of China. There would be no one who could break through. No one would be allowed in. As I began to just exist and deal with the dysfunction of my family life, I learned to survive by spending time alone.

Saturday was a day I would love and tuck away in my thoughts as my day. The day to escape and imagine a life much different from my own. My room was empty. The walls were bare, there were no posters or painted pictures. Nothing decorated with any love or care. My room had the bottom bed of a trundle bed with a mattress narrow enough to line a horse trough. I would lower my bed on the floor to stay cool at night. The walls exposed the wood frame and insulation that met with the plywood floor. There were two crank windows in my room that were taken from a trailer.

This perfect cool Saturday started like every other. I woke up and walked sleepily down the stairs to use the bathroom and then got right back up the stairs to my bed. If we got up before our parents

we would be beaten. The fear of punishment forced me to my room.

On my ascension to the top of the stairs, I was startled to find my mother and brother wrestling a rattlesnake. They, in turn, were startled to see me climbing up the stairs. We all looked at each other confused.

"What are y'all doing?" I asked.

"This rattlesnake must have come from the tree outside your window, crawled under your bed, and came to rest across the top of the stairs to find a cool place" they explained. "What are you doing?" they asked.

"I went downstairs to go potty and was on my way back to bed," I shared. This was my first impression and earliest memory that there was some angel or someone (must be God) watching out for me.

It was another Saturday. This day was not any different than any other day, except today my brother (15-years-old, 5 years older than I) thought I would make a great practice person for his pubescent desires. I didn't understand what he was asking me to do, so I went to him naively. He asked me to participate in unthinkable acts. I wasn't aware of what was happening. I didn't understand what he was asking. I did what he asked because he followed in his father's footsteps. He was a violent person, and I learned to submit.

Sitting on his bed, he began to try another position. At this time, I was determined to fight. He moved toward me and demanded that I take his parts in my mouth.

"This is not right, I won't do this," I yelled. His anger and violent expression forced me to partake in his god-awful demand.

What do I do? What can I do? I know! Bite. BITE HARD. You can get away and hide, I thought. Instinctively, I bit as hard as I could.

He flew across the room completely doubled over in pain, holding his parts while I ran with all my life to hide. To this day, I still have no idea how he didn't kill me. I can only imagine my imaginary friend "Jesus" hid me.

Another week went by. It was Saturday again. Saturdays had been the day I enjoyed, the day I escaped into the woods where I had a group of trees where I would live out my dreams and imaginations, where no outside world could come. These days were carved out as my safe space, but unrelenting darkness found its way there too.

It was one particular Saturday that created a crack in my great wall. The pieces of hard granite of my tough exterior, my self-protection, began to chip away. Sitting on the sofa, my older sister and I were startled to see our father walk down the stairs wearing only a white tee shirt and white briefs. He came to the couch and motioned to my sister to accompany him upstairs. To quench my curiosity, I proclaimed "I want to come too," to which he gladly allowed. I followed with anticipation that finally I would be joining in a position equal to my sister...being

accepted by my father. Was this the day I had hoped for? We approached his bedroom. As we entered, he removed his underpants and lay on the bed. My sister shyly sat away from me as he instructed me the way my brother had done.

A sense of shame flooded me. I was overwhelmed with confusion and disappointment. What was I experiencing?

What? How? Wait! WHAT? was all I could think.

I quickly got up and ran for my life down the stairs. I needed to get away. My sister met me outside. I looked her in the eye and asked, "Do you want me to tell anyone?"

Shaking her head violently, as to indicate to the shadow figure of my father in the upstairs window, "no" was her reply. But with her mouth cloaked by her hair where only I could see, she said, "Yes. He said I needed to tell you not to say anything or he would kill me."

The next day, with determination and finality, I went to the counselor's office in my elementary school and spoke to a lady who I learned shared my name, Rebecca Anne Smith (my maiden name). I walked boldly into her office. With resolve and focus (being only ten-years-old), I blurted out "You need to do something about this or I am going to run away," In two days, a sheriff and a Child Protective Services worker in a baby blue VW Beetle toting large black trash bags came to save us from our father.

Texas Baptist Children's Home Receiving home became my two-week respite from this nightmare. At the two-week mark, my siblings and I were placed in separate foster homes for four years. During this time it felt like life boot camp. Learning how to play the game and get what you want.

Texas Baptist Children's home in Round Rock Texas became my new world. For a year, this place was the adventure I had hoped for—along with two other foster homes until I was returned to my home. My mother and father had divorced, and she was promised if she got her own house, we would be returned. Unfortunately, I was the only one returned. My sister came for a time but was then moved to California. The next four years were full of the same disappointment of my previous life with my mother. The only difference was I was able to control my bowels. I was no longer considered stinky.

The despair and bone-aching feeling of loneliness, unwanted and utter disgust that I was alive, penetrated me to my current predicament. And so, I resumed my search for the thing in the garage that would help me end it all, but... couldn't find it. *I know I had it yesterday. I know right where I had it. Will I just do something right?*

A week earlier, my mother's new husband kicked me out of my house because he wanted to control me and hated that I was attending Christian events. When I called asking if I could go to a baptism he said "Well your goose is cooked the doors are locked and don't worry about coming home"

I sat laughing on my friend's bed (because I was taught not to cry). Then, my friend asked me if I wanted to get saved. Again, I thought I would be free. I said yes. Jesus became my savior. But my mother demanded I return.

That's when I decided to hang myself in her garage. I would prove to her no one has control over me but me. But I couldn't find the rope.

Suddenly, I heard the sound of the tires in the driveway. They were home. Startled, I looked at my hands only to discover that the rope had been in my hands the whole time. I fell to my knees and surrendered to God. He is my Father, my family, my hope, my acceptance. I had literally been saved!

When a caterpillar grows, it goes through a tough journey to become a butterfly. It climbs a tree, overcomes obstacles, and creates a safe cocoon to house its transformation. When it emerges, it has the fight of its life. It opens the cocoon only to physically press through the barrier to cause its new body to develop into what it was created to become. Each move causes the blood to push out the wings and the end result is the purpose and identity it was destined to become. This was me—the worm who had been through so much already that I was ready to accept the promise of a new beginning.

Shortly after graduating high school, I was determined to fix all the problems I had inherited and went searching for a candidate that would fit the bill. I was married at nineteen and began my new life in a new city and a new church. The hope that my life would change was at the forefront of my mind. I began to pray and question, "What is my purpose?"

"My Place in This World" by Michael W. Smith was my anthem.

It was Wednesday, and I was ready for the day, excited to be a part of the service and hear the gospel, eager to make others feel welcomed and loved. I sprang to my feet. There—I saw her. A beautiful lady sat in the back.

I have never seen her before, I thought.

Sitting down in front of her, I began to energetically explode with words of acceptance and stories of hope. This felt a little overwhelming to me, so I excused myself and sat back in the front row. Embarrassment and shame poured over me like hot lava.

What were you thinking? Seriously, you're probably going to scare her off like everyone else you've met in the past, echoed in my head. I left church desperately hoping she would return and that I wasn't a disappointment to God. I felt like God was the only one I hadn't disappointed, so in my new journey, I was becoming a perfectionist so as not to mess up.

It was Sunday morning, a new day to celebrate my new world and practice my new freedoms— like making my own decisions, talking to people and having them talk back, and feeling a sense of belonging.

I'm here. Is she here? Did I scare her off? Will I see her? ran through my mind.

Frantically searching, my eyes found her before I even realized it.

There she is! I thought, jumping with excitement. Being mindful of my new surroundings, I waited.

She approached and sat beside me, giving me a hug that went on for a long five minutes. "I am so glad you came and talked with me last Wednesday," she shared. "You see, I knew of this church. I heard it was a loving church. It was my plan to visit quickly, leave my son, and then leave. I knew the church would take care of my son once I was gone. I was planning on killing myself. But you came and sat with me, sharing so much and making me feel seen and loved. I realized I couldn't leave. As you can see, I didn't go through with it. Thank you."

Sitting, humbled, shocked, and so deeply touched, I exclaimed to God during praise and worship how grateful I was to have reached this one person, showing her the value that I felt when He saved me. Not long after this life-changing experience, the pastor approached me and asked if I would become part of the children's church team. My first time in the class was eye-opening. I had one child to teach, and I was petrified, not knowing if I would fail or teach the wrong thing.

It has now been over twenty years that I have had the privilege to pray over, love, and help both broken and whole, beautiful children.

My heart and desire in life has been to have children and give them a safe life filled with love and nurture, helping them achieve all they were created to be. I feel privileged to make a difference in the lives of children and help them see that they can, they are, and they will overcome any challenge they face. Most of all, I want to show them that God does care and love them no matter what—and that they have a purpose.

I have seen my children grow into amazing adults who are following their dreams. My husband and I adopted a sixteen-year-old (that's a story for the next book), and we have watched her change her stars. I am now a pastor for our children's church and have the joy of seeing the lives of children nurtured to become everything God created them to be.

REBECCA ANNE PRICE

Rebecca Anne Price is a woman that trusts God. In her search to pursue the presence of God she has encountered a multitude of opportunities. These opportunities have been to be a servant and a researcher. Her career has spanned from being a missionary, an administrative clerk in a hospital, Interim Director at a crisis pregnancy resource center, a researcher to establish SBA 8a status for a family therapist, nanny, jack of all trades. In every area of her career she has been a support to the companies she has been a part of. She is known in the business world as Techie Beckie because she finds and fixes a multitude of issues from data entry to computer challenges to lost items. She takes every opportunity to reach out and share her faith with those around her, helping others succeed in their pursuit of life.

It is Rebecca's hope to always continue to learn and Grow in God's word.

8

IT'S MY TURN

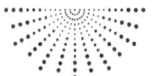

VANESSA GARCIA

*I*t was my Quinceañera, and I could feel my heart racing as I stood at the edge of the party room, peeking around the corner. I saw my family's handiwork—the decorations, the tables set with care, and the lights strung up to dance like stars. The air was filled with the soft rustle of dresses, and whispers of excitement. The music felt alive, pulsing through every inch of the room.

My mother and grandmother hadn't slept in days; they had bent over glue guns, glitter, and crepe paper in the late hours to get every detail right. Seeing all that effort brought to life for one unforgettable night overwhelmed me. When I finally walked in, seeing my friends, family, and even cousins who drove hours to celebrate with me, a warmth surged through me. This moment was for me, yet I couldn't help but think of the hundreds of details that went into making it memorable.

I remember sitting for a moment that night, letting it all sink in. My family was dancing, their faces beaming with laughter. It hit me then that I wanted to create this feeling for others—this sense of belonging and joy that filled the room. Little did I know that spark of inspiration would follow me through the years, even when life took me far from that first dream.

As I planned my wedding a few years later, I felt it again—that calling so strong I could hardly ignore it. I poured myself into every detail, wanting each moment to feel intentional, every flower and drape to speak to the love we were celebrating. For the first time, I hired an event planner. She managed the day, transforming my ideas into reality, and on the morning of the ceremony, I was surprised by how calm I felt. I wanted to be that person for someone else one day—the one who allowed a bride to savor her wedding day without stress, and just enjoy the beauty of the moment.

But soon enough, life stepped in, and I had to put that dream aside. My husband was a Marine, and suddenly, my life was swept into his mission, his duty. Years passed before I would fully understand what that meant.

Being a military wife wasn't just about loving my husband; it was about loving him from afar, separated by months, sometimes years, of distance. When we married, I hadn't signed up for a life of constant goodbyes, yet it soon became all too familiar.

Our first duty station was in North Carolina, and I remember the day we left Texas, a whirlwind of nerves and farewells. Standing at the airport, I hugged my family tightly, knowing it might be a while before seeing them again. My mother turned to my husband with a gentle but pointed look and said, "Take care of my daughter," before stepping back, leaving me with the heavy reality of what was happening. I was stepping into a new life I wasn't fully prepared for.

That first deployment was brutal. Shortly after we learned I was pregnant with our first child, he was gone. In my heart, I'd pictured us experiencing each step of parenthood side-by-side. Instead, I celebrated my son's first

Halloween, his first Christmas, and countless other milestones alone. Each deployment held its challenges, but the loneliness was a steady ache that never grew easier.

Over the years, we lived in California, North Carolina, and eventually, Okinawa, Japan. By that time, I was raising two boys in a country where I couldn't read the street signs, struggling to adjust to driving on the opposite side of the road, yet slowly adapting to this new, foreign life. I did my best to make the most of it—switching our currency to yen, teaching the children phrases in Japanese, and trying to create a stable environment amid the constant uprooting. Eventually, I felt confident enough to move us off base and into a rental home. But no matter how settled I became, my husband would leave again, for another stretch that was longer than the last. Even when he was home, his mind was often somewhere else, still wrapped in the demands of military time, while I tried to build a semblance of normalcy for our boys in a place where we were "the Yankees."

In time, the distance between us wasn't just physical but emotional. Years of raising my sons essentially alone had transformed me into a "single wife," a title I had never wanted or envisioned for myself. My mother had raised three children alone, and I'd once vowed I would never end up in her shoes. Yet, here I was —my dreams, career, and sense of self all sacrificed for a man barely around to share in our lives.

The military had its rhythm, which left little room for dreams that weren't adaptable to its clockwork. Each deployment pushed my ambitions further from reach, reminding me that my life was now on someone else's time. And so, I learned to wait.

For twenty years, I was a single wife, married to a man I loved, but I often felt separated by more than just miles.

Every goodbye stung a bit more, especially as my children grew old enough to understand that "Dad's leaving" meant he wouldn't be around for birthdays, holidays, and football games. Watching their eyes fill with tears tore at me, but I swallowed my heartache, letting them see only strength.

"We'll be okay," I would say, hugging them tightly. But inside, I felt broken.

One particular memory stands out—the typhoon. My husband was deployed, and we were living on base when I received an alert: a typhoon was coming, and I needed to stock up on essentials for three to five days. The familiar scramble to prepare kicked in, but a slow dread crept over me this time. I'd been through hurricanes before, but my husband had been there. Now, I was alone, trying to reassure two young children as the winds picked up and the rain began to hammer against the windows.

Power went out, leaving us in thick, muggy darkness - the sirens outside wailing into the night, shaking the building to its foundation. I could hardly sleep, clutching my children close, bracing for each gust of wind that rattled our walls. I rationed out our cold canned food for three days; whispering reassurances I wasn't sure I believed. When it was finally over, I remember feeling like I'd been in a fight, my body sore and my mind worn thin. This was our life now—a life I never expected, but one I was living for him, for our family.

I had accepted this sacrifice for so long as part of my chosen life. I had tried to be okay with setting aside my dreams, pushing them back into the shadows. But I didn't realize how much of myself I had lost along the way. As the years went on, I felt myself shattering, piece by piece. Each deployment took something from me: a sliver of hope, joy, and self that I didn't know how to regain.

One evening, alone in our tiny house in Okinawa, I looked out at the foreign landscape, filled with a suffocating sense of isolation. I asked myself, "Why am I here?" With no family nearby, few friends, and my husband somewhere I couldn't reach, I felt like I'd lost myself in this life that no longer felt like mine.

But despite the years, the setbacks, and the quiet strength that had carried me through, the dream to open an event planning business never faded. It stayed with me through each farewell, each long, lonely night, like a gentle whisper reminding me who I was and what I wanted to give to the world.

The breaking point came unexpectedly, like a sudden gust knocking me off my feet. My grandmother, the woman who had a huge role in raising me and had been my rock, fell seriously ill. Japan was twenty-four hours ahead of Texas, and I woke one morning to a message from my mother.

"Call me as soon as possible," it read. A sinking feeling weighed on my chest even before I picked up the phone.

"Vanessa, Grandma has pancreatic cancer," she said gently. "They're giving her three to six months."

My stomach churned, my pulse thudded in my neck, and my hands went clammy as I sank into a chair. Half a world away, the person who had loved me most was dying, and I had no idea how I would get to her in time. I contacted my husband's commanding officer, desperate to get leave to fly home. But to them, my grandmother wasn't "immediate family," and the request was denied. Guilt gnawed at me. How could I not be there for the woman who'd done so much for me?

After what felt like endless delays, I managed to bring the boys and get back to Texas. But the woman I'd always known—full of laughter, warmth, and unwavering strength—was a shadow of herself. She passed shortly after I arrived. I planned her funeral and returned to Japan, yet everything I'd built there felt suddenly unfamiliar. The grief, the guilt, and the hollowness of my life there all pressed on me, and I was once again a "single wife" in a marriage strained by distance.

A New Beginning

Looking back, I realize how much I sacrificed and how often it went unnoticed. At my husband's retirement ceremony, I sat in the audience, watching over a hundred Marines salute him, honoring his dedication, courage, and years of service. His medals gleamed under the stage lights, each a testament to his sacrifice. When they called me up and handed me a certificate of appreciation, I smiled at the cameras, but inside, I felt hollow. Was this slip of paper supposed to sum up twenty years of waiting, worrying, and raising our boys alone? I thought about my sons, how much they'd given up too, the nights they spent missing their father, and I wanted someone to see them, to recognize their sacrifices. But I knew it wasn't about us. It was his day and our time to move forward.

When my husband retired from the Marine Corps, it was like a weight I'd carried for decades was finally lifted. For the first time, we were no longer at the mercy of deployment schedules. On our road trip back to Texas, my husband and I were enjoying a quiet peace that felt like a long overdue holiday. The drive felt surreal as if it weren't just about getting home but about finding a new way forward.

At one point, we stopped for gas, grabbing snacks from a roadside stand, and my husband turned to me with a look I couldn't quite place.

"It's your turn now," he said with a calm but serious smile. "What do you want to do?"

His words filled me with a clarity I hadn't felt in years. I was no longer just a military wife, a single wife, or someone existing in the background. For so long, I'd held onto a dream—one I'd nearly forgotten—of creating something special for others, just as my family had done for me all those years ago at my Quinceañera. And now, finally, I could make that dream a reality. I decided to open my own event planning business in Taylor, Texas.

My grandmother always said, "Good things come to those who wait." Her words echoed in my mind, and I realized she was right. It wasn't my timing—it was God's. The journey had broken me and reshaped me, but it had also prepared me.

And finally, I was ready to step into the dream that had waited so patiently for me.

Starting a business comes with its own challenges. There were days when I felt overwhelmed and questioned if I could handle the weight of this new dream. But for the first time, the struggle felt worth it. I was doing something for me.

My first wedding for a client was a whirlwind of nerves, yet by the end of the night, as I watched the bride's family laughing and dancing, I felt the same rush of warmth I'd felt that night so many years ago.

It's funny how life works. For so long, I believed my purpose was to support others and be a constant in my family while my husband served his country. But I've realized I can still be that person while also pursuing my own dreams and successes. I'm learning that it's okay to be the center of my life sometimes—to choose my path and chase what makes me feel alive.

Owning this business has been a journey, a rediscovery of parts of myself I'd thought lost. I've learned that true strength isn't about always having it together; it's about knowing when to let go, ask for help, and say, "It's my turn."

As I look back on the years of sacrifices I made, I no longer feel like I'm drowning. I'm floating, maybe a bit wobbly, but moving forward with a strength and a purpose I never imagined I'd have. And that, to me, is everything.

VANESSA GARCIA

Vanessa Garcia is the founder of Sweet and Classy Events, LLC and owner of The Venue Taylor, Taylor, Texas's newest premier wedding and event space. A native Texan with a passion for creating flawless celebrations, Vanessa brings warmth, precision, and expertise to every event she touches, focusing on creating personal, unique experiences that bring families together and create lasting memories.

After twenty years of moving across the globe through six different duty stations with the Marine Corps, Vanessa finally planted roots in Austin, Texas, where she transformed her dream into reality. Today, Sweet and Classy Events is a veteran-owned business serving Austin and its surrounding communities.

Beyond her event planning work, Vanessa is writing about her journey through tribulation, betrayal, and sacrifice. Through her story, she hopes to inspire other women and military wives to persevere and pursue their dreams, no matter what challenges they face.

https://www.thevenuetaylor.com/
https://www.facebook.com/thevenuetaylor
https://www.instagram.com/thevenuetaylor/

9

BOUND BY LOVE, DRIVEN BY HOPE

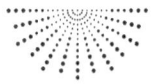

MARY PARKER

$\mathcal{A}$s I watch him celebrating with his friends—laughing and wrestling like boys, not yet men—a rush of pride fills me. He's overcome so much, more than any kid should, yet here he stands, strong and happy. Beneath the pride, though, there's sadness for what he had to endure and guilt—endless what-ifs. Is he truly okay? My mind never stops scanning for signs of trouble.

But then, I catch his smile—a warmth spreads through me like the sun on a Texas day. His laughter, his joy, fills my heart. Today, surrounded by friends and family for his high school graduation, I realize how close we were to a different outcome. So many nights, I wasn't sure we'd make it here, not with the mountains of obstacles that stood in our way. But we did, step by painful step.

He catches my eye as he excitedly talks with his friends about future adventures and college. His crystal-blue eyes lock with mine, and he tells me everything I need to hear with a playful, knowing smile. He understands. He appreciates it. At that moment, I know we are going to be okay.

But as I stand there, the memories creep in, uninvited but persistent. I see flashes of those darker days—the sleepless nights, the frantic phone calls, the times when I feared I'd lose him forever. I remember how his laughter disappeared, replaced by silence or angry outbursts. There were days when he wouldn't leave his room when the weight of his pain seemed too much for any of us to bear. We've come so far, but the shadows of what we went through still linger, reminding us how special these moments of peace are.

Growing up with a Navy stepfather meant constant moves for me and my five sisters. Every new town brought anxiety—would the kids like me? Would I fit in? Despite the worry, I forced a smile and adapted. The anxiety that felt like an elephant in my stomach eventually became butterflies.

I started M&M Babysitting Services at twelve, leaving a bag of M&Ms after each job as my signature. Caring for kids gave me purpose and helped me build connections with families.

But midway through my senior year, my parents announced another move—back to Groton, Connecticut. I was furious. Leaving my friends behind felt devastating, and I simmered in anger, refusing to make new friends.

At seventeen, I left Groton to follow my fiancé to Biloxi, Mississippi. I was ready for the uncertainty, armed with courage from every transition and challenge. Looking back, I see those constant changes built resilience. Each move taught me how to adapt and discover what I was capable of, and I slowly formed new friendships, even when I thought I couldn't.

After my fiancé left the Navy, we married and returned to Biloxi. I worked as a CNA at a nursing home near New Orleans, witnessing neglect and abuse. I couldn't stay silent, filing reports despite the nurses' hostility. I saw my grandparents in the elderly residents, and their stories of survival inspired me to protect them. My determination led me to advocate for those who couldn't speak for themselves despite the risks. That passion continued to guide me throughout my career.

At twenty-seven, I welcomed my precious son into the world, born at just thirty-four weeks and weighing a mere five pounds, ten ounces—so tiny I could cradle him from my wrist to my elbow. His arrival was fraught with danger; my blood pressure had soared to an alarming 200 over 150, leading to an emergency induction. During delivery, chaos reigned as our heart rates plummeted, endangering both our lives. Somehow, we emerged victorious.

This moment was the culmination of years of struggling with infertility due to polycystic ovarian syndrome (PCOS). From the age of nineteen, doctors told me I would never conceive, even suggesting a hysterectomy at twenty. Devastated yet fueled by determination, I refused to accept my fate. Again at age twenty-four, another doctor reiterated that I would never have children, I walked away, convinced they were wrong. I delved into research, seeking specialists who might offer hope.

Our lives changed when my husband received a job offer in Connecticut. There, I found a doctor at Yale who specialized in PCOS. He introduced me to vitamins and dietary changes.

At an insemination appointment, my doctor became concerned when he tried to insert a speculum into my closed cervix. I nearly jumped off the table from pain. Deciding to perform an ultrasound, he quickly realized I was a medical mystery: I was, in fact, already pregnant.

It was a difficult pregnancy, but every struggle was worth it. My little boy arrived perfect, happy, and smart. He was my world. I kept him close all day, carrying him in a sling as I worked, listening to his soft coos. He slept on my chest even at night, soothed by my heartbeat and warmth. As he grew, I loved watching him explore his world —climbing, painting, and playing. I rediscovered childhood through him, finding a happiness I'd never known. With his red curls, freckles, and mischievous grin, he owned my heart completely.

Then everything changed. At his eighteen-month check-up, I braced for the usual argument about shots. I couldn't understand how they could justify giving so many vaccinations at once to such a tiny child. That day, I insisted on only one, the DTaP. They relented after the usual back-and-forth, but agreeing to even that one shot would turn out to be the biggest mistake of my life.

My little boy looked at me, hurt in his eyes, as they gave him the shot. He screamed—and didn't stop. He cried for three days and nights, inconsolable. Nothing I did—my heartbeat, my warmth, his favorite foods—could calm him. He grew weak and listless, and I was terrified. Guilt tore at me. I'd caused this. Why hadn't I listened to my instincts?

On the third day, he had a seizure. My precious baby convulsed, his eyes rolling back, his body arching, and I was helpless. I hated myself, our doctor, and even God. I called the pediatrician's office immediately, but the nurse dismissed my concerns, insisting it couldn't have been the shot because the reaction hadn't happened within seventy-two hours. I was livid—I knew, without a doubt, that this all started with that shot.

From then on, my sweet boy was different. He went from walking, talking, and laughing to crawling, losing his words, and screaming in constant anger. The things he once loved only infuriated him.

Eventually, our pediatrician admitted he'd seen similar reactions in boys after the DTaP and MMR shots and wrote us a letter to excuse my son from further vaccinations. The office refused to support this, refused to file a claim with the vaccine injury program, and turned hostile instead. They bullied us, threatening to call child protective services if I didn't continue vaccinating.

Our doctor left the practice shortly after, rumored to have lost his license. I never confirmed this; my only concern was my child. He was my world, and watching him suffer with no support only deepened my resolve. From then on, I would protect him fiercely, no matter what anyone said.

A parade of professionals entered our lives: occupational and physical therapists, neurologists, and more. Instead of collaboration, their egos clashed, leaving me feeling mad at the system, exhausted, and constantly in pain. My son wasn't improving, and I feared he might be lost to us. Hitting my breaking point, I made a bold decision—I stopped working and canceled all appointments, channeling my anger into finding a better solution.

I sought out a naturopath who introduced a holistic approach, using vitamins and supplements to detox my son and heal his gut. I followed their regimen religiously, trying everything—zeolite spray, charcoal, hydrogen baths, and frequency healing. I became relentless, determined to reclaim my son. Slowly, he began to return to me. By age two, he was showing glimmers of the joyful baby I once knew, though still carrying some anger.

Throughout this struggle, I grappled with my rage toward the doctors and the system that had let us down. I realized that no parent should be coerced into medical procedures without informed consent. Every child deserves a caregiver who sees the whole picture and advocates for their well-being. If I could be that advocate for my son, perhaps I could help others, too. Little did I know just how much damage had already been done. But I was ready to fight back, turning my anger into a force for change.

As my journey to heal my son unfolded, my marriage began to crumble. Isolated in my fight, I felt a growing distance from my husband, who struggled to grasp the gravity of our situation. He favored quick fixes through medications, while I was committed to holistic methods. His absence at appointments and the long drives left me feeling unheard and invisible, fostering resentment as I carried the weight of our son's struggles alone.

My anger extended even to God; I believed I had been abandoned and punished for some unknown sin.

Desperate for answers, I returned to school. To provide medical insurance for my son's needed services, I started working again at a pharmaceutical company in New London, CT, where I quickly learned why I shouldn't trust the industry. I often found myself challenging the higher-ups, but I juggled my responsibilities, dropping my son off at daycare before work and studying after he went to bed.

Despite the chaos, my son was slowly finding moments of happiness. He played, walked, and talked, doing everything a three-year-old should do. Amid our struggles, a flicker of hope emerged, reminding me that even in adversity, progress was possible. I was determined to adapt and move forward, not just for myself but for my son.

Just when I thought life had settled, tragedy struck again. I was pregnant with my second child, elated from an ultrasound, eager to share the news with my son that he would soon have a baby brother. But as I approached the daycare, my heart sank at the sight of police cars and ambulances. An officer intercepted me before I could enter. His cold, detached demeanor only deepened the dread tightening in my chest as he confirmed my worst fear—a daycare provider had violently shaken my son. Six witnesses had reported it.

My stomach dropped. I felt like I was trapped in a nightmare, barely able to breathe, as they led me to my son. He was scared and crying but miraculously unharmed—or so it seemed. The officer pressed me for details about previous concerns while I stood numb, barely able to comprehend the horror unfolding before me. How could this happen? Why was my precious child being hurt yet again?

My son had no visible injuries, but his small, frightened voice broke through my shock: "My brain hurts." Those three words crushed me. I rushed him to the ER, where a CT scan confirmed a concussion. I was devastated, overwhelmed with guilt. Why had I trusted others with his care? I hated myself for working and for placing him in daycare. My self-blame was relentless. I raged against God, questioning why He would allow such cruelty twice.

The doctors offered little hope, telling me all I could do was wait and ensure he rested. But rest was impossible when my child often cried out from headaches and fatigue. Each day, the guilt deepened. I stayed home, consumed with researching concussions and dedicating myself to his recovery. My son's suffering became unbearable when, at just three years old, he pulled a push pin from a bulletin board and tried to harm himself, saying he didn't want to be alive. My heart broke all over again.

The rage inside me was volcanic, fueled by fear and desperation. I sought out every possible treatment—high-fat diets, oxygen therapy, and more hydrogen baths. Yet, the dismissive doctors insisted I was overreacting. One even suggested that I accept my son might end up on disability. I was furious. How could they be so heartless?

But I wouldn't let my fury consume me. Instead, I channeled it into action, fighting tirelessly for my son's healing. I was determined to navigate the despair and find a path forward—no matter the obstacles.

When my son started elementary school, I believed we might finally be on the right path. At first, everything seemed fine—he adjusted to his new routine, and I clung to the hope that the worst was behind us. But soon, the phone calls started. Behavior reports flooded in about anger outbursts, yelling at teachers, and lashing out at other kids. More unsettling were the frequent trips to the nurse's office, where he complained of debilitating headaches.

Fear gripped me once again. What if he was still suffering? What had I missed? Had we addressed the vaccine and head injuries or only scratched the surface? I spiraled into self-doubt, convinced I'd failed as a mother. My child was struggling, and I wasn't enough to help him.

Desperate, I sought out a neurologist. The headaches had lasted too long to ignore. Sitting across from the doctor, I heard the words that shook me to my core: head injuries can have lifelong effects. My knees rattled, my body shook as I held my son close. According to the reports, he had been violently shaken, and now I wondered if this turmoil would be our new normal.

The diagnoses started rolling in—seven in total by the time he turned six: Intermittent Explosive Disorder, Oppositional Defiance Disorder, ADHD, anxiety, and depression. None of them accounted for his head injury. I was overwhelmed, lost in the flood of labels. They prescribed medication, and I held on to a fragile hope that this might finally be the solution.

One day, while writing a paper for my psychology class, I got a call from the school. "Ms. Parker, we have a situation. You need to come immediately." I rushed over, expecting another fight, another incident of him standing up to bullies. But nothing could have prepared me for what I walked into.

Police and ambulances greeted me at the school entrance. My stomach lurched, and I fought back nausea as my legs threatened to give out. Not again. How could this be happening? Inside, my son was pacing frantically, fists clenched tight, his face contorted with fear. He kept shouting about blood on the walls, his terror palpable.

I rushed to him, scooping him into my arms, whispering that he was safe, that I was there. But he couldn't hear me, lost in his hallucination, pleading for someone to make the blood stop. His classmates had been evacuated, terrified by his outburst, and I was terrified, too. What was happening to my child? Where had this come from?

"Make it stop! Why is there blood coming from the walls?" he repeated over and over. The haunting words echoed in my mind as I held him tighter, rocking him back and forth. The paramedics, police, and social workers surrounded us, their presence a blur as I signed documents, proving that we were doing everything we could as parents.

Then, one of the paramedics—a kind woman, maybe in her sixties—pulled me aside. "We've seen this before," she said softly. "You should consider getting a different doctor for his medication." Her words hit me like a thunderclap. Here was this woman, risking her career to tell me the truth, offering the kindness of a grandmother in a moment of crisis. My cheeks burned with rage, my heart aching. I cried, and she held me while my son continued to ask why the blood wouldn't stop.

I had trusted the professionals, and yet here we were—my son lost in a nightmare and me, desperate for answers. But that conversation lit a fire within me. Something had to change.

I know you're wondering how I could have trusted these people or let this happen more than once. The truth is, I still blame myself for not seeing it sooner, for not taking action, and for not challenging the system that caused all of this. At the time, I was being yelled at, bullied, and harassed, constantly told that I was the problem. I felt utterly alone—my spouse was essentially absent, and I began to believe that maybe I was wrong. I was young and taught to trust doctors, to believe they wouldn't harm me or, especially, a baby. They made me feel like I was crazy, but I wasn't.

All the while, I was continuing my education, studying social work, child development, education, and psychology. At the time, I was completing my practicum hours at the Yale Child Study Center, where I had the chance to speak with the doctors who were training me. They helped me connect with a team that might have the answers I desperately sought about my son's troubling reactions. When they scheduled us with the genetics department, I felt a flicker of hope, like a door was finally opening.

The team was brilliant—intimidating, even—and after running genetic tests, they revealed a series of issues that would impact my son for the rest of his life. As they explained their findings, everything began to click into place. It was as if the puzzle pieces of our chaotic journey were finally starting to fit. I soaked up every bit of information, determined to fix this, to bring my son back to me, and vowed to protect him from anyone who might harm him again.

We modified our diets, detoxified our home, and started using different vitamins, neurofeedback, oxygen chambers—anything we could find that might help rewire his brain. It wasn't a quick or easy road. Our necessary dietary changes were so extreme that I leaned into my culinary training, determined to make nourishing and exciting meals for my kids.

And in the end, we got him back—well, mostly. At ten years old, he was diagnosed with PANDAS, a condition that causes neuropsychiatric symptoms following a strep infection. I'm convinced this traces back to the DTaP vaccine. To my shock, I learned that strep can be a carrier virus in many vaccines. When his symptoms flare—behavioral outbursts, emotional upheaval—I manage them naturally with supplements and vitamins. I've invested in neurofeedback systems, running protocols that help ease the emotional strain these flares bring.

Every step of this journey has shaped us. It hasn't been easy, but I am fiercely dedicated to protecting my son and ensuring he has the support he needs. This is where the pieces began to fall into place, weaving a tapestry of understanding from the madness of our lives.

Moving frequently as a child taught me resilience, helping me find the right people in the right places. Leaving home young forced me to grow stronger, forging a spirit of determination in the face of adversity. Experiencing and reporting abuse gave me the tools I needed to confront the challenges I faced in my own life. Working with individuals with autism and disabilities opened my eyes to the therapies my son would need. My culinary knowledge became a lifeline, equipping me to nourish him without causing harm. And my background in pharmaceuticals instilled conviction in my decisions, giving me confidence that we were on the right path.

The community around me—naturopathic doctors, advocates, mentors—became my support, each person a vital thread in the fabric of this journey. They helped rebuild my confidence, transforming the self-loathing I once felt into a drive to help others.

Looking back, I see now that every hardship laid the groundwork for the fighter I've become. He made it. *We* made it. It's going to be okay. My son graduated. He's happy, attending college, and working toward a bright future. He's becoming a healthy, productive adult equipped with the tools to navigate his past struggles. Together, we conquered the darkness. He knows how much I love him and that my world revolves around him and his brother. He understands that I will move mountains to ensure he has a good life. In healing him, I found my healing. Now, I'm on a mission to help others.

I no longer carry the weight of anger or blame. Instead, I've embraced God's path and committed to the work He's called me to do. Today, I help families through integrative mental health services, focusing on finding the root cause rather than masking symptoms. I refuse to accept the endless cycle of diagnoses that overlook the actual issues. Advances in science and technology have given us the tools to tackle mental health challenges to help families recover from vaccine injuries and concussions.

I've traveled to Washington, D.C., to advocate for children, opposing state policies that do not protect them. Alongside other warrior moms, I fight for my children and all children.

My kids are my why. They ignite my passion, fueling my fight for change. No family should suffer in silence, feeling isolated and alone in their struggles. God entrusted me with this journey because He knew I would tear down the mountain, stone by stone. He needed me to experience the pain, to see it firsthand. If I hadn't walked this path, I might not have believed in the power of resilience and healing.

Now, as I continue to pick up the pieces, I'm ready to share what I've learned, to light the way for others, and to ensure that no one has to walk this road alone.

MARY PARKER

Mary Parker is an integrative mental health professional, with fifteen years of experience in the field. She owns Infinite Potential Counseling Inc, located in Round Rock and Austin/ Dripping Springs. At Infinite Potential Counseling Inc, she is helping families identify genetic, diet and environmental issues that can impact mental health, and heal the whole person.

Mary is also the President of TX C.U.R.E. A non profit organization working with families who are impacted by the criminal justice system. Her role is to help foster and grow relationships for children and families who feel alone when a parent or veteran in their lives is incarcerated.

In her spare time, she is a homeschooling mom that enjoys hiking, kayaking, and traveling with her family.

Facebook: https://www.facebook.com/
infinitepotentialcounselinginc
Instagram: https://www.instagram.com/
infinitepotentialcounseling/
Twitter: https://x.com/InfinitepotenTX

10

THE MYSTICAL JOINERY

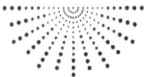

NATASHA CAMPISI

I stood in the empty garage, heart pounding, panic and shame tightening like a noose around my chest. I had been barely hanging on—three kids to raise, a career on the verge of collapse, and a mountain of bills that loomed over me like a dark, relentless storm.

The day my car was repossessed was the day I finally understood the depth of my struggles.

Walking into the house, my thoughts raced through the mess that had become my life. An imminent eviction was terrifying, the credit card companies hounded me daily, and the weight of looming bankruptcy pressed on me with suffocating force. I was drowning in uncertainty, and once again, the safety net I thought was there for me had unraveled.

Sitting on the edge of my bed while my children slept peacefully in the next room that night, I refused to let despair consume me. I had to push through—for them. Closing my eyes, I whispered silent prayers, hoping for a miracle, for any glimmer of hope to pull me out of this darkness.

A few days later, my phone rang unexpectedly. My manager's voice carried a hint of enthusiasm. "I'd like to invite you to dinner," he said. "There's a potential opportunity I think you'd be interested in." For a brief moment, it felt like the universe had heard my pleas.

That evening, I arrived at an upscale restaurant, the soft glow of candlelight starkly contrasting the chaos swirling in my life. My manager introduced me to Robert—a man whose charisma radiated from his confident smile. His words flowed effortlessly, and as he talked about business ventures, they shimmered with promise, like golden tickets to a better life. Sipping my wine, I felt a spark of excitement ignite, something I hadn't felt in a long time.

Yet, even as I listened, I questioned if something darker lay beneath Robert's charm. Why would someone want to be this kind with me? His interest in me seemed odd. I could sense his keen awareness of my vulnerabilities and his interest when I expressed my hopes for a new job with the subtle energy of desperation I knew I wasn't effectively concealing. I felt I was at a crossroads, teetering between caution and survival.

When Robert offered me the position of Executive Director, it felt like a dream. After years of struggling to rebuild after my divorce, this offer seemed like a victory. It meant financial security for my children and a chance to reclaim my identity and prove to the world that I was still capable and strong.

On my first day in the office, sunlight streamed through the floor-to-ceiling windows like a spotlight, signaling that this was my time. Everything gleamed with possibility—the polished desk, the leather chair. The horizon stretched wide outside those windows. I imagined a future where I could rise, lead with confidence, and fit the jagged pieces of my past back together.

Robert, charismatic and persuasive, had a way of making me feel invincible. At first, I reveled in his praise, which felt like a balm on my insecurities I didn't realize I had. He celebrated my leadership, and I felt seen for the first time in years.

But beneath my optimism, a quiet unease grew.

Over time, Robert's attention shifted. Late-night work texts grew more personal. Robert began using my vulnerabilities to tighten his grip on me. He knew my struggles as a single mother, he used it to draw me closer. His compliments, once reassuring, started to feel controlling.

"This is a partnership," he'd say. "We do this together." His words sounded supportive; I didn't realize he was pulling the strings, and I wasn't in control. I wanted to believe we were a team, but I feared to see the truth deep down. Robert wasn't my champion; he was manipulating me, learning my weaknesses, and building my dependence on him. And I let him, so desperate for stability.

Robert's attention became suffocating, but I was so indebted for all the help I accepted from him for my career, I couldn't escape his web. Many people I helped hire depended on me to keep them employed. Guilt and the promise of success kept me believing certain sacrifices are necessary. As time passed, I realized I was caught between ambition and manipulation. I had fought hard to rebuild my life, but now I stood on the brink of something far more unstable.

Months slipped by, and Robert's grip tightened and the lies began to surface. I discovered that Robert had fabricated the role of Executive Director specifically to lure me into working for him. He had painted a compelling picture of leadership and opportunity, but once I started the job, it became clear that something was off. Every time I tried to fulfill my responsibilities— managing his employees or making necessary changes to the business—he found excuses to block my efforts.

I later learned from his business partner that this was part of Robert's manipulative pattern: creating fake roles to entice women into working for him. Even the company name he used to hire me under was an old DBA that expired years prior. By the time I realized the truth, it was too late to just walk away. The pandemic had hit hard, and with no one hiring, I felt trapped. To make matters worse, my daughters and my best friend were already working for him, deepening the emotional entanglement. I was stuck in a situation I never anticipated.

The truth was very blurry; Robert had everything I sought in a mentor—insight, charisma, and an interest in my growth. I unconsciously clung to the father role he filled, which I had craved for as long as I could remember. In his presence, I caught glimpses of the love I had always sought but never found growing up. He guided me through the complexities of business, and I, dazzled by his brilliance, absorbed everything he said. He seemed to understand my ambition like no one else, and I admired the facade that masked the truth away. But it was all an act. Because my parents too played a confusing role in my life, the obvious dangers were cleverly hidden behind the familiar gaslighting I was raised in.

When I tried pulling away he planted doubts about my abilities and worth without him. "No one else will care for you like I do," he'd say, his voice thick with deceptive tenderness. "You need me. Look at the life you have now—because of me."

The evening began like so many others—casual and familiar, with conversation and laughter creating an easy atmosphere. But as the night went on, something shifted. Robert moved closer, and though I had once found his presence warm, it felt oppressive and smothering this time.

"You know how much I care about you," he said quietly, his tone darker than usual. His words carried an unsettling weight.

I felt uneasy but tried to dismiss it.

His hand is now on my waist, tucked under my shirt.

"This isn't appropriate," I warned, my heart racing as the space between us disappeared.

His eyes, once kind, now seemed predatory, making me feel small and powerless, like a child caught in a nightmare.

Then, without warning, he crossed the line I had fought to maintain. The man I had admired, trusted, and looked up to transformed into someone I didn't recognize. Before I could fully process it, he forced himself into a space that should never have been violated.

Everything I had trusted about him was shattered in that moment. The confusion and doubt I'd felt over the months were replaced by cold clarity— this man, whom I had seen as a mentor and protector, had betrayed me in the most devastating way. He sexually assaulted me. The betrayal was staggering, and realizing what was happening hit me like a tidal wave.

I pushed him away and stumbled out of the room, my body moving instinctively. Every step felt heavier as the weight of what had just happened settled over me. My world tilted, unsteady, as I tried to reconcile the man I thought I knew with the predator I had just escaped.

My understanding of trust and safety was destroyed

The assault crashed into my emotional body like an asteroid, setting off a catastrophic collision. It wasn't just an impact; it was a destruction so deep, that it felt as if the crater it created in me was deeper than any canyon I could imagine on earth. This wasn't just trauma—it was the unearthing of emotional tectonic plates I'd buried beneath years of survival. I'd tucked those feelings away, neatly hidden under the memories of doing what I had to do for my kids.

After a year of trauma-focused therapy, I understood what years of living in survival mode had done to me. I learned that trauma wasn't just an emotional wound—it had burrowed deep into my body, my mind, and my heart. It changed the way I saw myself, the way I moved through the world, the way I made decisions. The unresolved trauma from surviving had wreaked havoc for years, sabotaging me at every turn, making me believe I wasn't worthy, wasn't lovable, wasn't deserving.

Those beliefs weren't just whispers in the back of my mind; they were roots. Deep, twisted roots planted by abuse, abandonment, and emotional unavailability from my younger years. Realizing the depth of that damage was like picking up the first shattered piece of my broken self.

A few months after I completed trauma therapy, I felt a pull to grab my Goddess oracle cards from the top drawer of my dresser. Something told me to pick one. I shuffled, closed my eyes, and split the deck. When I opened my eyes, there it was, the Unconditional Love card.

I paused. I had to. The words stared back at me, but my body wasn't ready for them. My eyes welled with tears, my throat tightened, and my chest felt like it was caving in. It was hard to reconcile. I didn't feel worthy of unconditional love. Everything about my life felt contradictory to what the card was offering.

Unconditional love?

The path to unconditional love—of self, of others? Was I ready to venture into the depths of this question? A space in me that held so much pain...

I wasn't ready for her, but she came anyway, slipping into the quiet of my sleep like a shadow I couldn't outrun. She didn't arrive as some gentle guide or spirit, but as a mystical serpentine vine, winding her way through my body. I could feel her slithering up my spine, coiling through my nervous system, every twist sending a shiver through me. There was no escaping her—she touched every nerve, awakening a deep and primal curiosity within me. An alluring beckoning that intrigued my soul.

The Ancestral Grandmother spirit came to me—in my dreams.

Having worked with shamanic practices for years, I had already developed a deep respect for the wisdom held in the natural world of plant medicine. Ayahuasca appeared to me as a presence, woven into the fabric of the jungle scenes that unfolded in my sleep. The dreams were vivid and haunting in their beauty—lush jungles, ancient trees, and a presence I couldn't quite describe, but could feel deep in my bones. She appeared not as a figure but as a force, a maternal energy, both comforting and powerful. Each dream left me with a sense of profound curiosity and a feeling that something was shifting within me, beckoning me to listen.

At first, I didn't know what was happening. It felt like she was probing the darkest corners of my mind, finding the places I had buried for years, places I didn't dare to look at in the light of day. As she wound her way deeper into me, my fears —those old, buried terrors—began to rise. The nightmares started to take shape. They weren't ordinary nightmares. They were vivid memories of the past, disorienting, as if I were caught in a swirling, otherworldly vortex of life. Every fear, every unresolved trauma I thought I had outrun, suddenly burst to life, raw and unchecked.

The first time it happened, I jolted awake, drenched in sweat, heart pounding. It felt as though my body had been set on fire from the inside, lit up by this ancient vine, forcing me to feel everything I had been avoiding. Ayahuasca's presence coiled tightly inside me, whispering in the back of my mind that this was just the beginning.

The messages from my dream were loud and clear. It was my turn to pay Ayahuasca a visit. The ceremony began like any other—a circle of strangers, a Shaman drumming and chanting, soft candlelight, and the earthy scent of Palo Santo filling the air. As the medicine touched my lips, I knew my journey would be different. This wasn't the magical, life-altering experience I had heard others speak about in reverence. Ayahuasca came to me as a force, raw and unrelenting, pulling me into the darkest parts of myself. Almost immediately, I felt the descent. I was falling— tumbling down a rabbit hole into a disorienting reality where time warped and the air was thick with ancient sorrow. We traveled to my womb, a place I had long neglected, where the pain of unrealized dreams, heartbreak, and unspoken grief echoed. I wasn't prepared for what I found there—a lineage of suffering, twisting through my body, demanding to be seen.

At the bottom, I saw them—ghostly women from my ancestral line, each one clutching her heart, silently weeping in darkness. They were frozen in time, facing a light at the end of the tunnel they couldn't reach, trapped in pain that mirrored my own. The line was stopped but I was moving. *I* was the one called to break the cycle, to feel the pain they weren't allowed to feel. I was the one to release the chains, not just for me, but for all of them. The pain in their faces spoke but I couldn't make out the words. Their eyes were hollow and lifeless. I was bewitched to save them from the prison they lived in. My blood is their blood, their pain is my pain.

After the Ayahuasca journey, I felt like an exposed electrical wire, raw and alive with emotions. Like my ancestors, I'd been emotionally numb from pain but now I was feeling. The arcing of emotions was alive and raged in my body. I was terrified of the work ahead but intuitively knew it was necessary to understand the patterns that led me to become easy prey for predators like Robert.

I searched high and low for help in understanding the language of emotions.

One day I sat across the screen from my life coach, the Wheel of Emotions between us, its colors spinning like a child's toy. We'd done this exercise before—naming the emotions, tracing their roots—but today something heavier lingered inside me. I closed my eyes, feeling the familiar tightness in my chest, the knot in my throat. The emotion was fear, but it wasn't the kind of fear that made me want to run. It was deeper, more insidious. It was the fear of never being loved.

"What's the fear trying to tell you?" my coach asked, her voice steady but gentle, cutting through the silence.

I breathed in, letting the fear rise. It took me back to a familiar place, a childhood memory I had buried long ago. I was sitting alone in my room, my mother's absence louder than any words she could have spoken. She was there, but not really. Always just out of reach, emotionally distant, wrapped up in surviving an abusive marriage and caring for a handicapped son. I could feel the emptiness, the longing for her attention, her affection—a love that never came. And with it, the fear. The terrifying thought that maybe I wasn't enough, maybe I wasn't worthy of her love.

As I sat in that moment, something inside began to unravel. I had spent years avoiding this truth, convincing myself that her emotional distance was personal. But now, sitting with fear, I realized that wasn't true. The fear of not being loved by her had shaped so much of my life. It had crept into every relationship, every moment of self-doubt. It had become the lens through which I viewed myself—always questioning if I was deserving, always wondering if I was enough.

But then, as I traced the fear back, something shifted. I saw my mother's pain run deep, rooted in the absence of love from her father. Growing up, she never knew what it felt like to be truly cherished or cared for, as her father was mentally ill, abusive, and emotionally distant. His inability to show her love left a lasting wound, one that shaped her entire understanding of relationships. Without ever experiencing love, she was never taught how to give it. It wasn't that she didn't want to love—she simply didn't know how. Her emotional unavailability wasn't intentional, but a result of her own unresolved hurt, passed down through the generations. Her struggle to love me wasn't about me at all; it was about a little girl who never learned how to receive or give love because she had never been shown it herself.

As I began to trace the emotional trauma back through the women in my family, I saw how the cycle of pain and emotional abandonment has been passed down for generations. My grandmother, like my mother, grew up in a household devoid of affection, with a father who showed little tenderness and a mother too overwhelmed by survival to nurture her children emotionally. This left my grandmother with the same emotional void, and without the tools to express love, she unknowingly passed that wound onto my mother.

Each generation carried the weight of that absence, struggling with the same feelings of unworthiness and the inability to give or receive love. This legacy of emotional neglect wasn't just an individual wound—it was ancestral, repeating itself in the same patterns of detachment, abandonment, and survival. The women were all bound by the same invisible chains, shaped by their fathers' coldness and society's demands, leaving them ill-equipped to break free or rewrite the story. The exact image I was shown in my Ayahuasca journey was now making sense.

This generational wound created a lineage of women who weren't equipped to recognize abuse as abuse. Without a foundation of love or emotional security, we were all conditioned to accept neglect, control, and emotional unavailability as normal. Survival meant enduring—putting up with mistreatment because they hadn't been taught what real love or healthy boundaries looked like. Abuse, whether emotional or otherwise, became invisible, masked by the belief that this was just how relationships worked.

Without ever experiencing tenderness or being shown their worth, the women in my family developed a kind of numbness to cruelty. They internalized the message that their pain didn't matter and that enduring hardship was their role. This legacy left us all vulnerable—unable to see when we were being mistreated because we didn't know we deserved better. We couldn't name abuse for what it was because we had never known anything else. Breaking this cycle meant confronting the pain and redefining love, safety, and worth from scratch.

Robert's abuse, though painful, was a blessing in disguise. It shattered illusions I had about love, power, and worth, forcing me to confront the deepest wounds within myself. Through the heartbreak he caused, I was given the opportunity to reclaim more of my power and sovereignty—not by fighting against him and the pain, but by mending the broken pieces of my heart with the golden light of unconditional love. This love, rooted in self-compassion and forgiveness, became the foundation for healing not just my own wounds but those passed down through generations of women in my family. I know that my journey isn't just about me. It's about breaking this curse universally, helping others find the strength to heal their own wounds, and spreading the light of unconditional love that will free us all.

As I retold the story of my own life, rewriting the chapters of pain with love and compassion, I discovered the profound power that lies in reclaiming one's narrative. Through that process, I found my purpose. It became clear that my journey was not only about healing myself but also about guiding others—especially women—through their own transformative paths.

Today, as a narrative coach, I use narrative therapy to support women in rewriting the stories that have shaped them. I help them face the parts of their lives that once felt unchangeable, and together, we craft new narratives rooted in self-love, resilience, and compassion. This is the heart of my work: helping women reclaim their sovereignty by changing the stories they tell themselves, and in doing so, transforming their lives.

NATASHA CAMPISI

Natasha Campisi is an energy healer, empowerment life coach, and author who transforms lives through the power of storytelling. Her healing journey began in 2007 following a near-death experience, leading her to explore diverse spiritual and energetic practices including shamanism, reiki, Egyptian Ankhing, radiant heart meditation, and more.

Natasha's work blends these modalities to foster personal and spiritual growth.

She is currently focused on her most personal project: a novel about Iris, a hero born villain, who traverses timelines to retell her story to break free from the karmic cycles she has perpetuated.

Through her multifaceted approach, Natasha empowers individuals to heal and transform their lives.

https://www.natashacampisi.com/
https://www.linkedin.com/in/natashacampisi/
https://www.instagram.com/
sovereign_rising_11/

11

TREASURE ON THE BEACH

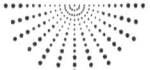

LISABETH "LB" THOMAS

y husband and I once seemed to have it all—a thriving ad agency, working with iconic Austin businesses, and a reputation for success in our community. But behind the scenes, he was a different man at home. His constant criticism and passive-aggressive behavior had eroded my spirit. I used to pray for God to give him a heart attack, hoping it might give him a change of heart. Eventually, I just prayed he'd have a heart attack, period.

To the outside world, I appeared confident, strong, and outgoing. But inside, I was riddled with self-doubt. I even second-guessed business proposals, always wanting to lower our prices despite knowing our creative strategies brought our clients success. I gave away ideas freely, only to see them show up later on TV or radio. Like my marriage, my self-worth was a fragile structure, constantly on the verge of collapse.

Years passed, and I finally reached my breaking point with my husband. We were a blended family with children who were best friends. We also had employees who relied on us, and clients we couldn't abandon. I was determined to avoid another failed marriage. But when it came to our divorce, his failure to file three years of taxes became the focus. Since I kept the business, he pleaded hardship with the IRS, leaving me with the bulk of the back taxes, interest, and penalties.

Then, as if life wasn't crumbling enough, within a span of three months, I lost my business, my home, and—heartbreakingly—my mom. I was shattered, homeless, and completely lost. I couldn't even bring myself to tell friends or the community what was happening. They knew about the divorce but not the depth of my despair. To them, I still looked like I had it together. Inside, I felt like a complete failure.

My three children were grown and independent, but they were heartbroken to lose our family home. I spent six months couch-hopping, with friends quietly slipping money into my purse.

Sleep eluded me, and I was consumed with anxiety. A friend asked if I was depressed. At the time, I didn't think so, but looking back—oh, I was deeply depressed.

I had gone from owning one of the best-known advertising agencies in Austin—producing films, TV shows, and commercials—to nothing. So, I lied. I plastered on a smile and pretended everything was fine while inside, I was dying. Every night, I'd lie in bed clutching a cheap bottle of wine (the grocery store bottom shelf kinda cheap) as my anger at God grew by the day.

"You could fix this in an instant!" I'd scream into the silence. "Where is my miracle?" But nothing came. Just more silence. Damn Him.

I knew at some point I would have to face my family, employees, clients, and friends and admit everything. My business had been my identity; now that it was gone, I feared what they'd think of me. Would I be friendless, too?

At my lowest, I couldn't speak without crying. My self-esteem had evaporated entirely. I'd sit there, silently berating myself—an idiot, a failure, worthless.

Then, one day, my friend Melinda invited me to her home in Galveston. I panicked. I had no money and didn't want to be a burden. But before I could refuse, she insisted, "We'll just walk the beach, eat what's in the fridge, and relax." So, I agreed.

That Saturday night, I told Melinda I'd get up at dawn to walk the beach alone. I needed to talk to God. The next morning, I slipped off my flip-flops and let the warm sand sift between my toes. The rising sun shimmered over the water like diamonds. For a moment, I forgot my troubles.

But soon, reality hit again, crashing like a wave. How would I pay my bills? What was I going to do with my life? Desperation rose inside me.

I had an idea, maybe something of value had washed up on the beach, so I started scanning the shoreline, hoping to find something—anything. "Come on, God," I muttered under my breath, "wash up something I can sell. A wallet, a money clip, an engagement ring —anything."

I walked further, my frustration mounting. I was angry and ready to give up. "God, show me the treasure on the beach!" I cried out.

And then, like a whisper carried on the breeze, I heard a voice I'd never heard before: "Oh, LisaBeth, *you* are the treasure on the beach."

I stopped in my tracks. It was as if time froze. I had been scouring the sand, looking for something valuable to save me, but the treasure I had been searching for wasn't outside—it was inside. I was the treasure. My worth, my value—it had been buried under the weight of loss and pain, but it had never been lost. It was still there, waiting to be uncovered.

At that moment, I realized the truth. I had been hiding from the world, but more than that, I had been hiding from myself. The treasure—the essence of who I was—wasn't something I could lose, no matter how much my life had fallen apart. It had always been there, waiting for me to rediscover it.

I returned to Melinda's house with a newfound sense of clarity. I couldn't hide anymore. I had to face my friends, family, and community—not to seek their sympathy but to reveal the truth.

As founding president of Texas Women in Business, I was asked to give a presentation at the holiday luncheon. As I looked out at the 200 faces—all expecting words of wisdom and humor from the one who had run a seven-figure ad agency, won awards, produced films and TV, worked red carpets, and interviewed movie stars —I thought, *oh God, what was I going to say? Could I say it? Could I admit all my failures?*

I stepped onto the stage and made sure my "all was fine" mask was firmly in place. But as I opened my mouth to speak, I paused, looked at my notes again, and said, "I have something to tell you."

For the next fifteen minutes, I laid it all bare—my failures, my struggles, my heartbreak.

I expected judgment, and when I only heard silence, I thought I'd received it. But then, applause and a standing ovation, I couldn't believe it. The outpouring of love and support overwhelmed me. The mask I had worn for so long crumbled, and I felt free for the first time in years.

Afterward, women lined up to share their own stories of hidden pain and struggles. It was at that moment I realized the power of vulnerability. Sharing my story had given them the courage to share theirs. But I also learned something else:

sharing your story to gain sympathy keeps you a victim. You become the victor when you own your story and walk through the fire.

Looking back, I see that time as both the most horrendous and the most wonderful of my life. It was when I finally had to face myself and ask, "Why have I been sabotaging my success? Why did I make myself small to make others feel big?"

I finally drew a line in the sand and said, "No more." At fifty-five, I was done playing small.

During this time, I had the opportunity to go through a personal development program called Discovery, thank God.

The first weekend, I let go of guilt, shame, and anger from my past. The second weekend, I realized my biggest fear was that I wasn't worthy or good enough. The third weekend, I focused on turning my hurts into purpose. After completing the program in 2013, I had the privilege of becoming one of their facilitators and the difference it made in my life was priceless.

I had no idea how much fear held me captive. Here was the thing, we're only born with two fears: falling and loud noises. Everything else we learn from family, teachers, social media, and the world around us. But here's the good news: if we can learn it, we can unlearn it.

So, how did I turn my life around? First, I had to face my fears and realize they weren't true. Then, I started paying attention to my self-talk. One day, I made a mistake and heard my inner voice say, "What an idiot! How stupid can you be?" My mouth dropped open—I couldn't believe how harsh I was with myself. I'd never talk to anyone else that way, so why was I saying it to me? I vowed to catch myself whenever that inner critic spoke up and say something positive instead, determined to change my inner critic into my inner cheerleader.

At first, I wasn't perfect, I slipped up but I kept at it. Eventually, the negative thoughts slowed and then stopped. Yes, I'm an exaggerator but I can honestly tell you that I don't remember the last time I said something negative to myself.

I'm now very aware of my two core fears. They were a part of me for as long as I can remember, but I don't spend time figuring out where they came from—that's in the past. When they pop up, I question if it's just my fear talking and remind myself, "I am worthy. I am good enough. And I am damn good at what I do." When fear rears its ugly head, I laugh and say, "Not today—I've got this."

Today, I'm in a wonderful relationship, starting our tenth year together. I'm surprised he put up with me in the beginning. My fears and distrust were over the top. I accused him of everything my ex had done, not once or twice but repeatedly. My fear-based thinking was pushing him away, and I knew I had to change or I'd end up alone.

I started paying attention to the negativity and accusations that came out of my mouth. One day on the phone, I stopped mid-accusation, realizing I was projecting my past onto him. I then told him to hang up and I'd call him back because I needed a do-over. He hesitated and said, "What?" I said, "Hang up, I need a do over," so he did. I called him back and instead of attacking him, I said as light-heartedly as possible, "Hey babe, how was your day?" We both laughed and the trajectory of our conversation completely changed. You know, sometimes we just need a do-over.

When my fears pop up now, I focus on the present moment. There's no fear in the present.

I was sitting by our pool recently, watching the sunset, and I started worrying about my deadlines at work, even though I was looking at the setting sun, I didn't see it. But then I reminded myself there was nothing I could do about the deadlines at that moment, so I shook my head and glanced back to the setting sun, and just then, dragonflies and hummingbirds danced all around me, I giggled as I watched them dip and dart all around me. I realized what I would've missed if I hadn't been in the present moment. Right then, my worry turned to peace.

My guy and I knew from the start we wanted something different, so we came up with a few rules:

1. It's not up to the other person to make us happy—that's an individual responsibility.
2. We'd never intentionally hurt each other, so we give the benefit of the doubt if something is said or done.
3. Give grace.
4. Kick a brick. If something hurts us, we speak up immediately, kick the brick to the side, to keep the wall from building.

Discovering my fears changed my life so much that I created a program called "Outwitting Fear." Through it, others can identify their core fears and recognize the triggers. The feedback I receive reminds me that we all have fears and stories. Some are more traumatic than others, but everyone's story is significant.

I'm blessed with three wonderful children and beautiful grandchildren. They're all successful, funny, compassionate, and happy. I felt guilt and shame for what they experienced for a long time, but I know it's never too late to change your life. We can be incredible examples to our children. Seeing our growth and transformation through hardship shows them they can face challenges and become the victor of their own lives. My children don't resent me—they are constants of love and support, and I thank God for them every day.

In every aspect of my life, I've never been happier. I'm grateful that my life fell apart because if it hadn't, I would have continued playing small and letting fear silently sabotage me.

The discovery of that treasure—my true self— didn't come without its struggles. But as I stand here now, I'm grateful for every moment of it. Because, as God showed me on that beach, I am that treasure.

Life may bury us under hardship, fear, and doubt, but our value never diminishes. It's up to us to dust off the sand, clear away the debris, and let our true selves shine.

The treasure isn't something we find. *We* are the treasure. And that's the greatest discovery of all.

LISABETH "LB" THOMAS

LisaBeth "LB" Thomas stands as one of Central Texas's most respected figures, renowned for her creative advertising campaigns and community leadership. As an award-winning producer, motivational speaker, and connector, she serves as Founding President of Texas Women in Business and *Not on Our Watch TX*, a statewide campaign combating child online sexual exploitation. Her influential work earned her the "Woman of Influence" recognition from the Austin Business Journal.

LB's journey to success emerged from profound personal challenges, including divorce, business loss, and her mother's passing. These experiences, though devastating, became the catalyst for her transformation. Through confronting deep-seated fears and rebuilding her life, she discovered her true resilience and purpose.

Today, she inspires audiences to uncover their inner strength and create transformative change in their lives, turning personal struggles into powerful testimonies of triumph.

My personal Facebook: www.facebook.com/ lisabeth.thomas.1
Outwitting Fear: www.facebook.com/ LBThomasBigCheese
OWF Instagram: Instagram
Personal website: LisaBeth Thomas – Speaker, Producer, Marketing Whiz Kid
Outwitting Fear website: Home Page - Outwitting Fear by LisaBeth Thomas
LinkedIn: https://www.linkedin.com/in/ lisabeth-thomas-985b581
Not on Our Watch website: Not on Our Watch Texas (NOWTX) - Protecting our Children

12

THE BEAUTY OF A LIFE

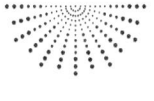

JULIE SMITH

I'll never forget where I was when the call came—the one that changed everything. It was a cold January morning in 1996. I had dropped my two-and-a-half-year-old son, Thompson, at my best friend Natalie's house. We traded babysitting regularly. Her little boy and mine were inseparable, and soon, we'd both have daughters—just three months apart. Life was as sweet as I could have imagined, almost like a fairy tale. I was the wife of a loving pastor, and we lived in a cozy parsonage right next to our church. I had always dreamed of being a stay-at-home mom, and now I was not only the mother of the sweetest little tow-headed boy but expecting a baby girl, too. We already had a name picked out for her: Laney.

Life felt full of joy and promise.

That morning, I sat in what would soon become Laney's room, sipping hot peppermint tea. Pale yellow paint had been picked out to match the soft pinks and blues of her flowered bedding. Tiny dolls and stuffed animals waited patiently along the walls for her arrival. As I looked around, my heart swelled with gratitude.

"God, You are so good," I prayed. "How could I ever thank You enough for all the blessings You've given me?"

At the time, I was leading a Bible study of forty women at our church. We were reading Kay Arthur's *Lord, I Want to Know You*, and I had just finished reading about one of God's names —*El Shaddai*, which translates as "God Almighty." My journal was filled with words of praise that day: "Thank You, God, for being all-powerful and providing for all my needs. You are faithful."

I was reading the chapter *El Elyon: The Most High God*, which specifically tackles the question of whether God "creates" or "allows" children to be born with birth defects— particularly addressing children born with spina bifida and Down syndrome—when the phone rang.

The chill outside was nothing compared to the coldness in the voice on the other end of the line. It was the nurse from my doctor's office calling with my bloodwork results. My AFP levels were high, she told me.

"That means the baby you're carrying likely has spina bifida. You need to come in today for further tests." The words landed hard, knocking the breath out of me. What? Spina bifida? I was just reading about it. But I had no idea what it meant. However, I knew it wasn't good.

My mind raced. "Could the bloodwork be wrong?" I asked.

"No," the nurse replied, her tone still flat and clinical. "Bloodwork is not wrong." Her lack of compassion shocked me. How could someone deliver such devastating news without a trace of sympathy?

I called my husband, David, who was working next door at the church. "You need to come home right now," I told him through tears. "We need to go to the doctor's office immediately—they think something's wrong with our baby." He was home in minutes, and we drove in stunned silence at first, then praying, "God, take care of our baby. We trust You." I kept repeating, "I just can't believe it. I just can't believe it. The blood work has to be wrong."

When we arrived, my doctor did a sonogram. After what felt like an eternity, he said, "Everything looks perfect. Sometimes bloodwork comes back wrong. There is no reason to be concerned." Relief washed over us. We were beyond grateful that there had been a mistake with the bloodwork.

"Of course, our little girl is fine," I thought. "God is sovereign. He is good." Still, our doctor wanted to monitor things closely, so I began getting sonograms every month.

Talk about an extreme range of emotions that day! I went from a peaceful time at home, sipping my hot tea and reading my Bible study, to hearing that my child might be born with a devastating birth defect, to everything being fine and no need for concern! Even though my husband and I rejoiced on the way home from the doctor's office, I still felt uneasy that everything wasn't okay with our daughter.

In the following weeks, I held on to believing everything was all right, but an uneasy feeling lingered. The Bible study I had been reading consumed me—particularly that section about birth defects. I thought, "Lord, did you bring this book into my life to prepare me for what's to come?" I desperately hoped not. Surely not. "God is good. He is faithful. My baby girl is perfect!"

I tried to push the thought away, but it persisted.

On May 22, at my thirty-five-week appointment, the atmosphere in the room shifted. My doctor's face grew serious during the sonogram.

I asked, "Is everything looking good?"

The doctor replied, "Uh, I want another doctor to look at this sonogram." And just like that, he left the room. He left me lying on the hard exam table with my husband standing next to me. We were completely silent. A tear slipped from my eye as David held my hand. We knew we were about to hear news that would change our lives forever. In what seemed like hours but was probably only a few minutes, both doctors walked back into the room with purpose and solemnity.

My world stopped. I could feel David's hand tighten around mine as the doctor traced a finger along the sonogram, showing us where her spine hadn't formed properly. I blinked back tears. This was not the story I had imagined for my daughter. She had spina bifida.

We left the office in a daze and drove to see a pediatric neurosurgeon. Along the way, David said, "I think we need to change her name to Bethany. It means 'house of miracles.' The place where God dwells. This is where God did a miracle, raising Lazareth from the dead." We knew God was still a miracle-working God. Her name needed to be Bethany.

At the neurosurgeon's office, we were hit with more devastating news. Not only did Bethany have spina bifida, but she also had hydrocephalus —a condition causing excess fluid in the brain. The doctor's prognosis was grim: "She'll never walk. She may be mentally handicapped. She may never sit up." His words cut deep, but what shook me most was when he added, "I'm sorry you didn't find out sooner so you could've taken care of the problem."

Wait! What? Do you mean to end her life because she isn't "perfect?" Was her life only worth something if she was created without "problems?"

I replied, "She is perfect, just the way God created her to be." As I watched this self-proclaimed atheist roll his eyes at my statement, I knew. I no longer wondered the answer to the question in chapter four of my Bible study book —God had created her precisely as she was meant to be. And whether He created or allowed her condition didn't matter—He is still good. Not everything that happens to us is good, but He is good. "And we know that God causes everything to work together for the good of those who love God and are called according to His purpose for them." (Romans 8:28)

I don't have the words to explain the peace that came upon me in the doctor's office after hearing the specialist's life-altering news. Not the peace I had that morning while drinking my hot tea before receiving the news. But true, deep peace— not based on circumstances. If you've ever experienced peace that passes all understanding, you know it's real and only possible through Jesus.

We called our family and shared the news, and everyone began praying. We informed our church family, and as you can imagine in a small Texas town, news spread like wildfire on a scorching day. We began receiving calls and letters from people all over the United States. Many offered their condolences, and many offered words of encouragement. We even received articles from medical journals about what to expect when raising a child with spina bifida and hydrocephalus. We did not read any of those articles. We either threw them away or filed them for a later time because we knew this was not the time to prepare but to pray. If the time came when we needed to know everything, we would learn then—but not before.

The following weeks were filled with prayer. Hundreds of people gathered to lift Bethany up, believing God would perform a miracle.

On June 11, 1996, our families were in my hospital room, praying and praising—nervous, excited, and yet, a little solemn. For many weeks, I had been reminding God that this would be a great way to display His power and that many would grow in faith after witnessing such a mighty miracle. Would God heal her like we fully believed He would? Would God perform a miracle and prove the atheist doctor wrong?

Would I have a story to share of God's miraculous power for all to hear and believe? I would know the answer soon!

The cold, sterile hospital room buzzed with activity. There were more doctors and nurses present than I could count, prepared for the baby they assumed would be born with spina bifida and hydrocephalus, a baby who would need immediate care. I remember looking up at my husband, who had tears in his eyes. This should have been the most exciting day of our lives, welcoming a little girl into our family and making our soon-to-be three-year-old son a big brother. The day that God would do a miracle.

I asked my husband, "Do you think God healed her?"

He said, "I don't know." We knew we would know in the next few minutes.

Did God heal her? I could not imagine that He wouldn't. After all, I knew He was good, He loved to heal, and I had faith way bigger than a mustard seed, as the Bible speaks about in Matthew 17.

The minute the doctor said, "She is beautiful," I knew her face was beautiful, but her back was not. Her back was open, and her spinal cord was exposed, with nerves unattached. She had the most severe case of spina bifida/hydrocephalus, called myelomeningocele. She was not healed.

Why? Did God not hear my prayers? Did He not hear all the prayers of the hundreds of people praying for her healing?

The flurry of activity in the operating room made my head spin as the doctor began sewing me up and handing my precious one to the multitude of doctors. I couldn't hold her because her back was open, and they had to wrap her up and decide what to do next. I just could not believe she wasn't healed.

I soon found myself back in my hospital room, without my baby, when a hospital representative came and explained that my daughter would need to see specialists (urologists, neurologists, orthopedists, and many more) every six weeks for the next several years. Those appointments might eventually be expanded to every six months for the rest of her life.

What? I had no idea! I had not prepared for this! I had been praying for healing instead of preparing. Maybe I should have prepared! I didn't know what to do!

I wrestled with the disappointment and shock of this news. But amid the heartbreak, something miraculous happened. A deep peace settled over me—a peace not based on circumstances but on the unwavering faith that God was with us. I trusted Him. I didn't need to prepare—He would give me everything I needed when I needed it. I knew He would, and He did.

Bethany underwent a five-hour surgery that same day to close her back and insert a shunt to drain the fluid from her brain. The doctors did what they could, they "stuffed" the nerves into her spinal cord, but they could not reconnect the nerves. Only God could do that.

The first Sunday I returned to church after Bethany's birth, we sang "Great Is Thy Faithfulness." As I stood there, holding my precious daughter, tears streamed down my face as I choked out the words that came from deep within my spirit, singing as I had never sung before: "Great is Thy Faithfulness! Great is Thy Faithfulness! Morning by morning new mercies I see; all I have needed Thy hand hath provided, Great is Thy Faithfulness, Lord unto me!"

The new depth of understanding of God's faithfulness and goodness overwhelmed me. He did not abandon me or my precious daughter. He cradled me in His arms as I cradled Bethany— gently, carefully, lovingly. I had never felt the love of the Father at such depth before. I had experienced the peace that comes from the Creator—the One who is good, who is love, who rejoices when we rejoice, who cries when we cry.

Raising Bethany has been anything but easy. She's had sixteen surgeries. She's faced physical challenges, learning struggles, and moments of exclusion. Has it been easy when kids made fun of the way she walked or when she faced external and internal health struggles? No. Has it been easy when school was hard for her? No. Was it easy when she was laughed at or left out of groups because her spina bifida made her different? No.

But she's also defied every expectation. The doctors said she wouldn't walk, yet she runs. They said she might be mentally handicapped, but she graduated from Baylor University.

I don't understand why God didn't answer my prayers for complete healing. But I trust Him. He is sovereign. He is good. He never left me to figure things out on my own. He directed my steps. He gave me what I needed exactly when I needed it. He even provided the book I needed to read and the thoughts I needed to consider before I learned of her situation. He was the God that flooded me with peace when it didn't make sense to have peace. Only God could do that. He is compassionate, caring, faithful, loving, and good.

I understand and believe with my whole heart that God has a purpose for Bethany's life. Just like she has a unique fingerprint, He has a unique purpose for her life that could only be accomplished in the way God made her. Life is short, whether we live one day or 100 years. This world is not my home. It is not Bethany's home either. I want to live my life on purpose, for the purpose God has for me. To love God and to love others. I love God not because He heals. I love God because He first loved me, in all of my ugliness, in my sin, in my unbelief, at my worst. He has a plan for my life that is better than I could imagine.

In Isaiah 55:8-10, the Word says, "For my thoughts are not your thoughts, neither are your ways my ways," declares the Lord. "As the heavens are higher than the earth, so are my ways higher than your ways and my thoughts than your thoughts."

I will forever trust in the Lord Jesus, and know that He is good, and maybe, one day, when I'm in heaven, I might ask Him, "Why?"

But, I have a feeling that I will fall on my face in gratitude that He was with me every step of the way and that He chose me to walk this priceless journey of knowing Him more fully in my pain, my hardships, my questioning. I sought the Lord, and He answered. I trust Him.

"You will seek me and find me when you seek me with all your heart." Jeremiah 29:13.

Through Bethany, He has shown me the beauty of a life created for a purpose far beyond what I could have imagined.

JULIE SMITH

Julie Smith is a Certified Christian Life Coach and Human Behavior Consultant. As the founder and CEO of Relationalities, she is known for her passion and expertise in helping individuals, couples, families, and teams strengthen both personal and professional relationships by uncovering their divine design and unique wiring. As a frequent speaker at women's meetings, conferences, and marriage retreats, Julie draws on her extensive background in education, sales, ministry, and human behavior to offer transformative insights and practical strategies for growth. Julie's greatest joy is being a wife, mother, and grandmother, married to her husband, David, since 1989. Her deep desire is to empower others to walk in freedom with their Creator, who has a plan filled with hope and a bright future.

www.Relationalities.com

julie@relationalities.com

https://www.facebook.com/julie.t.smith.96387/

https://www.instagram.com/
julie_thompson_smith/?hl=en

https://www.linkedin.com/in/julie-smith-
018638327/

13

DIAMOND IN THE ROUGH

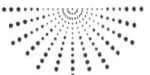

DEBORAH OWEN VALENTINE

The old wooden bridge creaked beneath me as another tear splashed into the murky ditch below. The night air was cold and still, and the only sounds came from the frogs and crickets in the marsh. Their steady songs were like a lullaby that eased the tremor in my chest. Above, stars glimmered, pinpricks of light, like promises from a faraway place.

Here on this fragile bridge, I could let go. Here I wasn't that scared, little girl. Here I could feel something close to peace.

"God," I whispered as I tilted my head back towards the sky, my voice barely more than a breath in the cool night air. "Why did you put me here? What did I do to deserve this? Why doesn't anyone love me?"

The stars didn't answer. They never did.

Tears fell silently into the deep ditch below. I cried for everything—for the girl I was, the girl I wished I could be, and the woman I feared I'd never become. I cried for the love I'd never felt, for the safety I didn't know how to find, and for the hope that, despite everything, I still clung to like a lifeline.

Behind me, our small house squatted in the darkness like a crouched beast. More skeleton than home.

Abuse and dysfunction were woven into the very fabric of our lives. It was in the walls, in the silence between screams, lurking like a predator ready to pounce. Our house was small. Its walls bore the scars of my father's rage—holes punched through the drywall, each one like an open wound. Cold air slipped through those cracks, wrapping itself around me like a cloak of despair. The back rooms were half-built dreams, my father's abandoned project. The old floors smelled of damp wood rotting from the inside out. Sunlight peeked in where it could. Rats gnawed at the wood and roaches crawled in the darkness while I tried to sleep. The walls were bare with weathered paint.

The familiar sound of breaking glass shattered the night's peace, followed by Mother's muffled cry. Empty bottles clinked against each other in the kitchen trash. My father reeked of beer and sweat, his clothes like a second skin drenched in neglect. By sunset each day, his words slurred into growls. I had four brothers, but the one just two years older than me was my rock.

When I'd ask my mom if we'd always live like this, she'd say, "Let's wait and see." Those words hung in the air like false promises, heavy with the weight of tomorrow. But tomorrow never brought change, only more of the same. My older brother worked part-time after school, earning enough money to give him a small escape from our reality.

There was no escape from that house, not yet. My mother wasn't going to leave Dad, not with four kids and nowhere to go. Then came the day that shattered what little safety I had left. My mom wasn't home at the time. I walked into my room and found him there—my father—lying naked in my bed, his hand on himself, calling me closer. My heart stopped. The world stopped. I ran, legs shaking, sobs choking me. I crawled under the house, in the belly of the beast, hiding in the cold, damp dirt, praying he wouldn't find me. I prayed that God would let me disappear. The fear was so suffocating.

A few days later, Mom took us to my Aunt's house. For a moment, I felt safe. My cousins were there, and I had someone to play with to distract me from the nightmare of my life. But even that was temporary.

Then came the day that broke me: Mom said we were going back home. Back to that monster. My heart shattered, the pieces sharp and jagged inside me. I begged her, "Please, don't take me back to him."

But it didn't matter. We were going back.

Back to the dungeon. Back to the nights when I lay curled in a ball, trying to stay awake, praying he wouldn't come for me again. What was I supposed to do now? We were back in that dark, suffocating house.

In the middle of all this waiting, my brothers and I became survivalists in our own home. We all carried the scars. As we grew older, the weight of what we lived through followed us like shadows. The deep-rooted sense of worthlessness didn't fade; it only grew louder, whispering lies that became harder to ignore.

"Please let me die," I whispered to the darkness. I was a ghost in my own house, haunting, a place I couldn't escape. My sadness and loneliness clung to me like shadows, always there, always watching.

I had one close friend, and I stayed at her house whenever I could. I felt like I was in a fairy tale. The house was bright, clean, and peaceful. There was laughter, music playing, people talking to each other and laughing, and a warmth I didn't know at home. I would sit there, soaking in the calm, wishing I could stay forever. This must be what love looks like. Maybe they would let me come live with them. Oh, how I wanted to live here.

At almost sixteen, it was time to start junior high school.

Oh no, what will I wear? I wondered. *I don't have nice clothes like the other girls.*

One Saturday, my older brother grabbed my

hand and said, "Come on. We're going downtown."

The excitement bubbled up inside of me. The bus dropped us off right in front of Foley's in downtown Houston. The warm summer breeze felt fresh on my skin. As we walked inside, my brother said, "Let's get you some clothes for school."

My heart soared. I picked out three dresses and a pair of shoes, treasures that held the promise of a different life. He put the clothes on layaway. But not long after, he brought them home. I finally had something to wear that made me feel seen—really seen. I walked into that school with my head held high. For once, the world didn't seem so heavy. People talked to me, friends I'd never had before. One of the football players asked me to be his girlfriend and wear his letter jacket.

Suddenly, I was somebody, but that feeling came with a price. I realized early on that looking good was the only way to feel like I mattered. I even became a cheerleader for a while, a bright spot in the sea of darkness. But the reality of our situation crept back in when I couldn't afford the cheer uniforms or the twirler outfits. There was no escaping the truth. The life I dreamed of was always just out of reach.

Love seemed like the answer. At sixteen, I married my childhood sweetheart, dreaming of safety, of gentle hands and kind words. He treated me like a princess, bringing me food when I was hungry and staying by my side when I was sick. But how could I love him when I couldn't even love myself? It was hard to let him touch me. Whenever we lay in bed, the memories of my father would flood back, making me feel sick inside.

I soon grew restless. I realized I was too young to be married, so we divorced. Then I did the one thing that I said I would never do, I moved back home, back to my parents, back to the nightmare. I started hanging out with people who weren't good for me, people who'd already been in trouble with the law. I smoked cigarettes, I partied, and I slept; anything to numb the pain.

The Army man came next, with his baby-blue GTO and sky-blue eyes. His smile felt like sunshine after endless rain. We married quickly, and I moved with him to Killeen. For a while, I thought I'd found my fairy tale—until the day I found the drugs hidden in my car.

"What the hell is this?" I demanded, my voice trembling.

His face changed—darkened, almost. Before I could react, his fist connected with my jaw. His gun's cold barrel pressed against my back as he hissed, "Shut up."

The next morning, when he went back to base, I packed my things and drove straight to Houston, pregnant with my son.

Eventually, I remarried my first husband, had a daughter, and tried to build a life. Again feeling bored, I got a job with the airlines, and for the first time, I felt free. Back then everyone dressed up to travel. Men wore suits, and women looked elegant in dresses and heels. I was part of that world now, traveling the globe, and feeling respected, and I thrived on it.

But soon, I wanted more freedom. I moved out with my kids and divorced my husband for the second time. I started leaving the kids with babysitters or their dad as often as I could. Dancing became my new escape. I'd dress up, go out, and get lost in the music. I even had a pilot write a song about me once!

The world seemed full of possibilities, and it was, but not for someone looking to fill a crater-sized hole inside of them. I never stopped to realize that the hole was getting bigger every day.

Then Mom got sick. Cancer ate through her like acid, leaving nothing but bones and pain. My aunt and I took her to the hospital, hoping for the best. After the surgery, the doctor's words hit like bullets: "She has six weeks to live at best." I couldn't accept it. Not my mom. She wasn't going anywhere. But just two weeks after her diagnosis, she was gone.

I lay on my sofa for a week straight, ignoring the phone, ignoring the knocks, ignoring my own beating heart. I felt lost, sad, and disbelieving. I floated through life like I was in space, with no beginning or end.

Then my brother's voice cut through the fog; "Come to California. Bring the kids. Start over."

The waitressing job in California felt like a mockery of my airline days. Each shift was endless coffee pots and sticky tables, a constant reminder of how far I'd fallen. That's where he found me—the dealer with the too-bright smile.

He'd sit in my section every day, watching me with knowing eyes.

"You look tired," he said one evening, leaning against the counter after closing. "I've got something that helps."

"I don't do drugs," I said, but my voice wavered. He knew I was lying.

He smiled. "This isn't drugs. It's just a pick-me-up of sorts. Something to help you get through those long shifts."

The first line burned, then blossomed into beautiful numbness. Suddenly, the world seemed manageable. The pain dulled. The memories faded. I could work, exist, and breathe without feeling the weight of everything I'd lost. Before long, he started charging me for it, but I didn't care. The powder became my new God, my morning prayer, and my nightly confession.

When summer came, I sent my daughter back to Houston to spend time with her dad. By the end of summer, I called to say she was better off with him.

They deserve better, I thought to myself. *They deserve more than your broken pieces.* I didn't even think about how that crushed my little daughter, who needed her mom.

A few months passed, and I decided to send my fifteen-year-old son back to Houston to live with his stepdad. Just before boarding the plane, he sat his suitcase down and turned towards me.

"Mom," he called out, voice breaking. "I'm coming back." I turned away, too numb to feel the weight of his sadness.

However, I started to look back at Texas. California was becoming dull now that reality had set in and my cocaine addiction had worsened. I decided that if I moved back, I could fix things, but my addiction packed its bags and moved with me. Back in Texas, I moved in with another dealer. Her two-story house looked respectable from the outside, but inside it was all darkness and paranoia. I ran deliveries to pay for my habit. One night, three police cars tailed me through Houston's back streets. My heart pounded as I made turn after turn, their headlights steady in my rearview mirror. I barely made it to a friend's house, hands shaking as I flushed everything down the toilet, watching the powder disappear.

Friends warned me I was dying. I could see it in the mirror - hollow eyes, gray skin, but death seemed easier than feeling again. I had become mean and uncaring about anyone or anything. I hated everyone. I was out for myself and didn't care who I hurt or what it took to get what I wanted. I ignored them and continued on my path of destruction.

Driving one day, I felt an unusual urge to visit Lakewood Church. Sunday came, and I went to Lakewood. Later that day, my mind drifted back to the warm feeling I had just experienced at church: An awakening of a truth I had known from childhood, no doubt arising from my grandmother's Christian influence. I began to pray and ask God to help me, for him to take the urge to do cocaine away. I wept from the very depths of my soul. My heart felt as if it was breaking into a million pieces. I pulled out my Bible and began reading it. As I read about Jesus, the urge to fill this emptiness became stronger. I cried out to God for months to change me and take the urge of cocaine away. I continued to read my Bible and pray for God to change me.

When I opened my eyes one morning, sunlight streamed through my window differently, somehow cleaner and brighter. I sat up, confused by the lightness in my chest. The mirror in my bedroom showed me something I hadn't seen in years—eyes that sparkled, skin that glowed. I ran cool water over my face, staring at my reflection in amazement. I walked to the kitchen, almost dancing and looking out the window. I started thanking God for whatever this feeling was, tears rolling down my face.

My son was now in the Navy in San Diego, and my daughter was married to a wonderful man. I was still broken and alone. My relationship with my kids was strained. I'd hurt them so badly. I formed a relationship with my daughter, but my son refused to let me back into his life.

Then came that Friday night. Someone told me about a special church. A place of healing and being set free.

"It's like a hospital for broken souls," they told me.

I don't even remember walking in.

The music washed over the crowd as people cried; there was such freedom, people were singing and dancing. It should have seemed strange, but something about that atmosphere touched me when nothing else could pierce my heart.

After the preacher finished preaching he called those up who wanted to be prayed for.

That's when she found me—the woman who held me without a word. She embraced me without question. She didn't offer advice or judgment. She just wrapped her arms around me and held on while I shook. Years of pain poured out of me like blood from a wound. I cried until my throat was raw, until my legs gave out, until the tears ran dry. Her embrace felt like everything I'd been searching for in powder and pills—safety, acceptance, and love without demands.

That night when I got home, my sheets smelled different—sweet, like spring flowers. Sleep came like a gentle wave instead of the usual cocaine crash. When I opened my eyes the next morning I saw it—the baggie in my drawer.

Just looking at it made my stomach turn. I picked it up, expecting the familiar surge of need, but felt only revulsion. The powder that had been my lifeline now looked like the poison it was. I shut the drawer and figured the urge would hit me later that day. When the sky started to darken I pulled it back out. It was like looking at a plate of food after eating a Thanksgiving feast. I simply didn't want it anymore. I flushed it without hesitation, watching it swirl away. A weight lifted from my chest as it disappeared.

Later that day, a friend came by with her familiar mirror and line. The mere sight hit me like a physical blow, turning my stomach.

"No thanks," I said.

"Come on," she coaxed. "Just a little pick-me-up. You look like you could use it."

I shook my head, amazed at the certainty in my voice. "I'm done."

She left, confusion written across her face. But I knew. Something had shifted inside me, fundamentally and forever. The craving that had ruled my life had vanished like morning mist in strong sunlight. Not just the need for cocaine but the desperate emptiness it had filled. I was free.

A few days passed, and I began to realize my prayers had been answered. I laughed, I cried, and I thanked God again and again. There was hope for me after all. I had distanced myself from my family and surrounded myself with users and dealers, but now I knew I could change. I could heal.

Like a diamond formed under extreme pressure and heat, all that pain had transformed into something else—something clear and hard and precious. The bitterness just faded away. This bitter shell of a woman had become something beautiful, something that could reflect light instead of absorbing darkness.

Years later, on a quiet Texas night, I found myself walking out under a vast blanket of stars. The air was sweet with jasmine, and somewhere in the distance, the crickets sang their familiar songs. I stopped and tilted my head back, letting starlight wash over my face.

"Thank you," I whispered, and this time the words came easy, wrapped in gratitude instead of grief. The same stars that had witnessed my despair now sparkled like diamonds themselves, reflecting the light I'd found within my own transformed heart. Standing there, I remembered that girl who used to beg these stars for answers, who felt so worthless, so unloved. I wished I could reach back through time and hold her, tell her that grace would find her, that all this pain would be transformed into purpose.

A cool breeze stirred the trees, carrying the scent of wild honeysuckle. I closed my eyes and smiled, remembering how that first night of freedom felt, how my sheets smelled sweet and my heart felt light. The memory was no longer bitter. Like everything else in my life, it had been transformed into something beautiful, a testament to the power of grace.

I took a deep breath and opened my eyes. Above me, the stars continued their ancient dance, no longer silent witnesses but old friends, twinkling with shared secrets of transformation and hope. I was home—not in any building made of wood and walls, but in my own healing, in my purpose, in the endless Texas night that had seen me through both darkness and dawn.

DEBORAH OWEN VALENTINE

Deborah Owen Valentine, a native Texan residing near Austin, brings a rich background of professional and spiritual leadership to her community. After beginning her career as an airline ticket agent, she spent twenty-one years as a leasing consultant in real estate, managing comprehensive office procedures for various residential properties including homes, townhouses, and apartment complexes.

Deborah's true passion emerged through her devoted church service, where she progressed from assistant leader to leader of Women with Purpose. Her spiritual journey includes serving as a Ministry Team leader, participating in healing rooms, the Flag and Dance team, and completing Prophetic Ministry training.

Now married to the love of her life in Elgin, Deborah serves alongside her husband on their church's Pastoral Team. She dedicates herself to empowering and supporting women through their spiritual journeys, helping them realize their God-given potential.

14

POWERLESS TO PEACEFUL

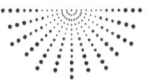

DEANNA COX

*A*nother surgery? We sat in the doctor's office, snow falling outside—a rare sight in Texas, especially with temperatures below thirty degrees. Inside, it felt stuffy and hot. I struggled to breathe, panic creeping in. This was the third or fourth surgery in the last ten years—I'd lost count. A torn ACL at thirty-five? My husband, Peter, had played football in high school, but this injury wasn't from sports; it was from a fall—either off a ladder or the truck's tailgate. Every time he got hurt, we ended up in the emergency room, and this was no exception.

"Are you sure, Doctor? Does he need this surgery?" I asked, barely keeping the anxiety out of my voice.

The doctor, an older man with kind but stern eyes, was shorter than I'd expected. His tanned skin and dark hair made him look out of place in the cold. "He's torn his ACL and will continue to be in pain unless we repair it," he said matter-of-factly.

We were at one of the top orthopedic surgeons in Dallas. Trust wasn't the issue—it was the pain medication.

"How much pain will he be in after the surgery?" I asked, my mind racing to the past.

The doctor hesitated, slightly taken aback. "Quite a lot. We'll insert a bulb of morphine for the first day, and after that, we'll prescribe painkillers."

Morphine? I was shocked. Did the doctor know about Peter's past? Probably not—why would Peter have told him?

"Doctor, do you know about his addiction?" I pressed.

The doctor nodded. "Yes, we're aware, and we'll monitor him carefully."

His answer didn't comfort me. I knew the pattern that had brought us to this point. I knew how easily Peter could slip back into the darkness.

Sunday was a day of worship. Our family always went to church, sitting in the same area with family. Growing up in church, I had always had a relationship with God. I was taught to pray, ask for forgiveness, and live a Christian life. But the pain of Peter's addiction and abuse slowly eroded my faith. We continued to go to church, going through the motions, but it felt like God wasn't there for me. Why would He allow my family to suffer through this? To become stronger? That's what I'd been taught. But I didn't feel stronger; I felt defeated, unworthy, and stupid.

I became the woman who believed in God but didn't feel deserving of His love because of what was happening in our home. Over time, I stopped praying daily and drifted away from my relationship with God. Peter stopped going to church altogether.

Many Sundays, after fights that left him ripping the sleeves off his sports coat or throwing things like a child, the kids and I would go to church and then escape to my family's lake house after lunch. As they grew older, my children went to friends' houses. I went anywhere else but home.

The summer following the ACL surgery, Texas was in the midst of a heatwave. Our yard was overgrown, the pool was turning green, and the house was falling into disrepair. This wasn't how we lived—until now. Peter had always been the type of man who could fix anything, the kind of man who could take a Q-tip and a cotton ball and build something extraordinary. But since the surgery, he wasn't the same.

Hours passed, and I wondered why he was still in the travel trailer. What was he doing in there? And why was there always a foam cup on top of the refrigerator? Curiosity got the best of me, so I walked out to the trailer.

There he was, sitting at the small table with another foam cup in front of him. His expression was distant. He was separating the ingredients in the hydrocodone pills. Soaking them in a small amount of water to separate the codone from the other ingredients. My stomach dropped. Who does this? How does he even know how? Why would anyone?

"What are you doing? What's in the cup?" I asked, my voice shaking with disbelief.

Peter didn't look up, his response sharp and dismissive. "What's it to you?" His tone made it clear—he felt no remorse.

Now, I knew the truth. He was buying again. Our lives had already unraveled—cars repossessed, bills unpaid, Peter not going to work. And now, we were losing our home, our friends, our sense of normalcy—all because of this addiction.

At the grocery store, I saw an old friend I used to chat with regularly. I smiled and said hello. She looked at me but kept walking, her expression cold, distant. This kept happening with different people. It felt like the world was turning its back on me. What had we done to deserve this? Why were people treating us this way?

Finally, I reached out to a friend who hadn't abandoned me. She told me the truth: Peter had been stealing, buying drugs, and asking for money—claiming it was for me. For me? Why would he say that? What lies had he been telling?

It was then that I saw it. Peter wasn't the man I had married. He was once kind, loving, and responsible. But addiction stole him, and I was too blind—or too hopeful—to see it clearly. I stayed because I wanted our marriage to work. I had been divorced before and didn't want to fail again. I participated in things with him I would never have considered without his manipulation. I was ashamed of what I'd allowed to happen in our home. After years of lies, manipulation, and abuse, I knew it couldn't continue.

One Saturday morning, much like any other, with children around the house, the last straw came. My oldest was away at college, my second child, seventeen, had left for work, my daughter, twelve, and our youngest, seven, were watching TV in the den. I had just gotten out of the shower when it all started.

Peter stormed into the bathroom, already in a bad mood, upset I'd woken him with the shower noise. His words were sharp and cruel: "You are so fat; why don't you go on a diet? I can't even look at you. Why did you let yourself get fat?"

I looked at him, said nothing, and walked past him into the bedroom. He followed, continuing, "Are you going to answer me? You always look like crap! I should have married someone sexy and pretty, like my ex-wife. You look like a slob! Where are you going?"

I answered softly, "I have four children; that's why I'm fat."

But I thought, *I'm not fat. I'm barely over five feet tall and might weigh a hundred pounds.*

He grew louder and angrier. "Where are you going? Are you taking the children? I have things to do, so they can't stay here."

Finally, I let my anger out. "Are you going to buy drugs? Is that why you're being so mean this morning? Are you out?"

He grabbed my arm and swung me toward the bed.

My daughter came to the bedroom door, knocked, and asked if I would come out to get them breakfast. She knew. She knew what was happening.

I went out to the kitchen, face distraught, and poured bowls of cereal. I looked at her and told her to use the safe word. It broke my heart that she even had a safe word for when things got bad at home. She called her dad, who picked her and my youngest up pretending to take them for softball practice.

My ex-husband and daughter had devised the safe word. It was a way to get them out of the house without having to deal with Peter. My ex always took my youngest, too, even though he was Peter's child. He had a soft spot for him and took him every time he took our daughter somewhere.

After they left, Peter, now dressed, was still raging. He continued, saying anything he could think of to hurt me—insulting my children, my family, my work, my appearance, my worth. He boasted about cheating on me, anything to make me mad enough to keep fighting. I took the laundry upstairs, and he followed. Our stairs were steep and carpeted. I was putting away clothes in one of the bedrooms, and he kept at it.

"Why do you do all this for these children? They don't need these TVs, and we need the money. I'm selling them all today and their game stations, too!"

He knew how much this infuriated me—selling my children's things to buy drugs. I turned and shouted, "You are not touching their things! Sell something of yours or steal something, but you will not take anything of theirs out of this house!"

He had succeeded. I was furious, and now he had a reason to be irate with me. "Don't talk to me like that! I paid for all this and will take what I want when I want! You have no authority to tell me what I can do in *my* house! You'd have nothing if it weren't for me!"

I knew I couldn't win this. He would only get meaner. I turned to go downstairs. He grabbed my arms and shook me as I walked past him out of the bedroom door. Now, I was scared. I was crying, begging him to let me go. He was always cruelest when he didn't have his drugs. He continued walking us toward the stairs. At the top step, he let go of me and shoved the laundry basket at me. I lost my balance and tumbled down the stairs like a rag doll.

He stood at the top, looking down at me, laughing. I was shaking, my body aching. I knew I was hurt.

He stood at the top, looking down at me, laughing. I was shaking, my glasses broken, and a cut across my nose, likely from the glass or my fingernail. He came down the stairs, stepped over me without acknowledging my fall, and walked to the other side of the house.

I heard the front door open and quickly went to the pool table, pretending to fold clothes, unsure who had come in. My second son was stopping by the house to grab something before heading to his girlfriend's. My voice was shaky, though I didn't think he noticed anything was wrong. I said hello and asked what he was up to. He went upstairs, came back down, said goodbye, and mentioned he'd be home later.

I barely held it together while he was there. Once he left, I broke down in tears. I heard the door shut again. Peter had gone out. He returned later in a much better mood. He'd been to see his dealer.

Not long after that "last straw" event, I sat in my car on a sweltering July day, suffocating under the heat and the weight of my family's expectations.

My mother, who'd seen enough, stood at my car window, shouting, "Why don't you just leave? You know if you stay, you're only hurting your children!"

I shouted back, "I want to leave, but it's not that easy. I don't have the resources to walk out!"

She grew louder, angrier. "You're letting him hurt you and the children! I thought you were smarter than this!"

I wanted out of the marriage, but I didn't know how. I knew they would help me, but I feared feeling indebted to them.

Her face turned red with anger as she gripped my car door. "You let yourself be controlled, even though we all told you to leave a long time ago! This is your fault—you're destroying your children! This is not how I raised you! I raised a strong woman who would stand up for her family, especially her children. That's not who you are anymore. Do you even care about them? Should they come to stay with me for a while? You're not thinking about anyone but yourself! You're selfish!"

Her cold stare pierced through me, and I started to cry. I couldn't breathe or think straight. Tears streamed down my face, and before I knew it, I shouted, "I'll kill myself! You take the children and raise them—I won't destroy them anymore!"

The words hung in the air. Then I saw my daughter sitting in the passenger seat, her face a mix of shock and fear.

"No, Mom! Don't do that!" she screamed, her voice shaking, tears pouring down her face.

That was the moment everything hit me. I couldn't let this go on. My children needed me, and I had to take control of them and myself.

When we got home, my daughter called a friend to escape the chaos. My youngest son was at a friend's house. My children had developed ways of coping—finding any distraction from the turmoil at home. I went straight to the bathroom and looked in the mirror. I didn't recognize myself. *Who are you?* The face staring back at me was thin, pale, tear-streaked. I collapsed to the floor, sobbing. How had I let things get this bad? How would I ever get us out of this?

After what felt like hours, I pulled myself together enough to sit down with my Bible. I had strayed so far from God that I didn't even know where to begin. I opened to Psalm 23: "The Lord is my shepherd." I had heard those words countless times, but now they felt different. I needed a shepherd, peace, and Jesus back in my life.

But how do you find your way back when you've strayed so far?

Going to the bank was one of the hardest things I'd ever done. I walked in, feeling small and defeated. Our banker, a man we'd known for years, greeted me kindly, but I could barely hold it together. I broke down as I explained that we couldn't pay for the house and that I was leaving Peter. Tears, sobbing, the whole thing. I was mortified, but he understood. He gave me time to get settled before they took the house.

Peter volunteered to return to Iraq shortly after we moved into the rental house. It wasn't surprising—leaving was his way of escaping reality. His addiction never stopped; it just found new forms. I filed for divorce before he left for Iraq. The divorce wasn't finalized until his return. This was my way out, and I took it.

Life slowly began to take shape. My children and I rebuilt a sense of normalcy, even though it was a new kind of normal. We moved away from Peter's church and back to the church I grew up in, settling into a new routine. Healing took time, but it came.

At first, I felt closer to God. I felt like I was home. That feeling didn't last, though. Even though we were divorced, some church members still saw me as connected to him. I was shunned to the point I stopped going to church, or I'd sit in the back of the balcony. I continued to drop off my ten-year-old son and fifteen-year-old daughter until she started driving. They always went to Sunday School and youth church. My oldest boy, twenty-one, completed trade school and started a family; my middle son, nineteen, was in his first year of college. Both were in different parts of Texas.

A few years later, I met someone special. He is a gentle soul, a calming presence in my life. We'd known each other when we were younger, and reconnecting felt like a gift. He treated me with the respect and love I had always longed for. We married and started going to a church where we both felt at home.

Despite these new beginnings, I still felt unsettled. My work was successful, yet we struggled financially. My heart was heavy, my marriage strained, and deep down, I knew I wasn't entirely myself. This had nothing to do with my current husband. It was because I hadn't forgiven myself or let go of the time I allowed someone else to destroy my world. I hadn't fully reconnected with God.

One day, driving home, a tightness gripped my chest. I felt like I couldn't breathe. The discomfort was so severe I thought I was having a heart attack. My heart raced, my vision blurred, and my palms were sweating. At urgent care, they told me it was a panic attack. Another wake-up call—a sign that something wasn't right. It was one more way God was trying to get through to me, but I hadn't made a habit of listening closely.

I sailed past the signposts God had placed to redirect me. When He spoke in a whisper, I ignored Him. Trying to do things my way without surrendering to His guidance was why I felt unfulfilled and reactive to life instead of being led by Him.

It took me twenty years after my marriage with Peter ended to fully reconnect with God. I had started attending a women's Bible study called Rooted, and it was there that I felt God's presence again. I had been going through the motions for years—working, surviving, going to church, and providing for my family—but I hadn't truly been living. I hadn't been rooted.

But God never gives up on us, and since He couldn't get through gently, He made His guidance more obvious. One day, as I was leaving the grocery store, a woman tried to pull into my lane and nearly hit me. I was already having a rough day, and that was the last straw. I threw up my hands, shouting through the windshield, "Seriously? Do you even know how to drive?" It wasn't like me to react this way, but I justified it. It had been a trying day, after all.

I drove a block before guilt hit me like a slap. I knew exactly what it was—it was Jesus.

He was saying, *Go back and apologize. Go back!*

I knew I had to listen. Tears poured down my face as I turned the car around. When I pulled up beside her, I got out, still crying, and apologized. At first, she looked shocked, but then her face softened, and we talked for a while.

That night, in my Bible class, the lesson was almost too perfect. One of the leaders said, "When we don't listen to God on the small stuff, we get comfortable drowning out His voice for the big stuff."

I felt as though she was speaking directly to me. God had been trying to get my attention for years, and I hadn't listened. He had to "slap" me awake, but now I could hear Him loud and clear.

This moment of listening and following God's promptings led to more clarity in my life and ultimately filled the emptiness I'd felt for so many years. Little by little, I took action by tuning into the guidance I was given and learning to listen to the nudges before they became a proverbial slap.

Recently, when offered a job that would have been a financial promotion but required me to move, I knew my answer. Praying about this, I believe Jesus answered me and this was a "carrot" not worth chasing. The more I pray and connect with my family, community, and church, the more I identify what truly matters. I chose to prioritize quality time with the people I love over money. It's not about wealth or past regrets; those things won't matter when I'm gone. I want my legacy and my purpose to be that of a woman who walked with Jesus.

This year, I was honored to be elected Events Chair for the Austin chapter of the National Association of Women Business Owners, where I connect with other heart-centered women and support the growth of their businesses. I also launched Premiere, which consults with restaurants and small businesses, helping them expand, build corporate credit, and secure the financial footing to succeed. My Bible study group continues to strengthen me as I walk through faith and community. Max and I are on the right path; my healing has deepened, and our relationship has grown. All my children have families of their own now, and each walks with Jesus.

Every day, God reveals to me that the most joyful way to live is by serving others, walking in peace, faith, and purpose, and helping others see that God works through us—even if we have to hit rock bottom before we finally hear Him. My hope is for a legacy of peace, love, and faithfulness. By God's grace, I have found healing, and now I share my story to help others find their way through the fire to a place of peace, a place with Jesus.

DEANNA COX

Deanna Cox is a business consultant, corporate credit specialist, public speaker, author, foodservice expert, and co-owner of Premier Business Consulting. With over twenty years of experience and a heart for faith, family, and community, she possesses a passion for helping businesses flourish by making a positive impact in life and business.

Deanna's journey began with early exposure to commerce through her grandparents' business, developing her innate ability to connect with people and understand their needs. This foundation has made her a dedicated advocate for business growth and success across industries.

While her professional accomplishments are impressive, Deanna remains firmly rooted in faith and family. She is married to Max, has four successful married children, and is a grandmother to nine. She enjoys time with family and friends, volunteering, and the outdoors. Her legacy is one of empowerment, peace, love, and faithfulness.

Connect with Deanna: LinkedIn: linkedin.com/in/deannacoxtexas

15

SEEING THE LIGHT

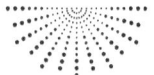

BY DR. CINDY STEWARD

From the moment I entered the world, I was sick.

My parents told me that I had high fevers almost constantly, along with infections, colds and the flu. I was continually throwing up and had seizures, ear infections, headaches, strep throat, tonsillitis, constipation, diarrhea, failure to thrive —the list goes on. My body struggled just to survive. I couldn't eat, couldn't keep food down and even sleep was rare because of the constant pain. This went on for the first two years of my life.

The doctors told my mom she wasn't producing milk in the first few days after my birth. They said I needed formula, and my mom, trusting the doctors, agreed.

But here's the truth: All mothers produce colostrum for the first three days before their milk comes in. Colostrum is like liquid gold for a newborn's immune system. It's packed with nutrients that build up the baby's defenses, but I missed out on that vital start because the doctors didn't explain how beneficial colostrum is for the baby. They made her feel inadequate, like her body wasn't providing what I needed, when in fact it was doing exactly what God created a mom's body to do; make colostrum rich milk to nourish a newborn. Also, the more a mother nurses her baby the first the days with colostrum the more milk she will produce later.

Instead, I was put on formula. My body didn't handle it well at all. I was allergic to the formula they gave me, which led to terrible colic. My belly swelled with gas, and I screamed for hours. The formula sat in my stomach, undigested, souring in my gut and damaging the lining of my intestines because I couldn't digest it. My mom believed the doctors when they told her formula was better than breast milk but in actuality every formula is inferior to mom's milk. The formulas are made with toxic ingredients causing inflammation. My poor parents were at their wits' end, questioning if they could ever handle having more children after the ordeal they were going through with me, their firstborn child.

THE FIRST STEP TO FINDING RELIEF

For two years, the symptoms persisted. The doctors were out of ideas, eventually recommending exploratory surgery to find the source of my issues.

But just before they went down that road, a friend of my dad's said, "Take her to a chiropractor first."

My dad was really worried about the idea of a chiropractor adjusting his baby girl. But not wanting me to endure surgery, he decided to give it a try.

After just a couple of adjustments, my symptoms disappeared. The vomiting stopped. The seizures and fevers faded away. I wasn't getting sick anymore, and I could finally sleep through the night.

It seems almost too good to be true, right? How could a chiropractic adjustment have made such a difference? Well, at the time, it was standard practice to put mothers under anesthesia and then pull the baby out. The doctor had tugged me into the world, twisting my head and neck which threw the first two vertebrae in my neck—the atlas and axis, entirely out of alignment. These two little bones are critical because they protect the spinal cord and allow the body's life force to flow freely. When misaligned, it disrupts the signals between the brain to the body and from the body to the brain so the brain doesn't get the full story of what is happening in the body.

When Dr. Stith, my chiropractor, adjusted me, it was like turning the lights on. I don't remember those early adjustments, but I remember Dr. Stith—a chain smoker who would puff away between adjustments. Cigarette smoke aside, he was my chiropractor until I was ten years old, and I loved going to see him. He changed my health (except maybe the cigarette smoke).

My dad, a farmer working for the Santa Fe railroad, was so impressed by the difference chiropractic care made in my life that he decided he wanted to become a chiropractor himself. But there was a problem—money. He didn't have the funds to go to chiropractic school, and with my parents working full-time to support our family, it took years before they could make it happen. Finally, when I was in the sixth grade, he was able to enroll. The very next semester, two of his brothers joined him in school. Both of my parents worked full time jobs while dad went to chiropractic college. They worked hard and it was exhausting. I remember helping my dad study by drilling flashcards with him. Today, more than twenty-one family members are chiropractors, including my daughter and me.

NATURAL HEALTH AND NAET

Chiropractic saved me, but the damage from those first two years didn't completely disappear. My stomach and intestines were still a mess. Food still made my tummy hurt and swell because the good bacteria were gone and the bad bacteria took over. Plus, I developed food sensitivities because of leaky gut syndrome. I also had migraines, and terrible pain with my periods that caused me to miss school and work. It took years of searching for answers before I finally found relief.

I became obsessed with learning more about health. I earned a bachelor degree in biology and another in nutrition. Eventually I became a naturopathic doctor focusing on healing through natural care rather than drugs.

My body reacts the opposite of how medications are supposed to work for people. Medications only seemed to make my symptoms worse, so I pursued natural solutions, and that's when I came across Nambudripad's Allergy Elimination Technique or NAET. I flew to California to become certified and, during my training, discovered I was sensitive to over fifty different foods. Fifty! We stopped counting at that point and just got to work on treating the sensitivities.

I had spent years dreading eating because of the pain and bloating that followed every meal. When the intestinal lining is messed up it can't digest the food and it spoils and ferments, which caused me to look like I was nine months pregnant within a half-hour of eating. Now, it is so nice to be able to eat and not hurt.

NAET gave me my life back. It wasn't a quick fix, but it was worth it, and since then, I've helped hundreds of my patients overcome their food and environmental sensitivities using the same techniques.

RETRAINING THE BRAIN

Athletics was never my strong suit. While some people are naturally athletic I struggled to catch or hit a ball. I wanted so badly to be on a team. I'd stay after school to practice, but no matter how hard I tried, I couldn't do it. The teachers were great. They knew how hard I was trying and they were baffled about why I couldn't do these simple things.

Even when my kids were little I'd try to help them with baseball skills but my son would eventually say, "It's okay, Mom. We'll wait for Dad. You're going to get hurt."

That's how bad I was.

Then, I met Dr. Brimhall and attended one of his seminars. He asked for a volunteer to come up on stage so he could demonstrate his technique. I couldn't get my hand up fast enough. He chose me and I went up on stage and climbed onto the treatment table. He shined a light in my left eye and asked if I could see it.

"No," I said. "There's no light."

For the next hour and a half, he worked on retraining my brain and eyes using all the neurological techniques. It turned out my eyes weren't working together, which made it hard for my brain to track anything. This explains my lifelong struggle with sports. After that session, I could finally see the light.

Now, I have all the advanced tools at my disposal —lasers, hyperbaric oxygen chamber, Trifecta Healing Bed, Right Eye testing / treating equipment, Balance Tracker to test and retrain neurological systems and equipment to help improve neurological function and increase the quality of a person's activities of daily living. Our new EESystem will be a huge boost for everyone. Each piece plays a role in helping my patients regain their lives, whether they're recovering from concussions, autism, or brain injuries.

Concussions were something I was all too familiar with, too. I've fallen off horses, tumbled down stairs, crashed on bicycles, fallen out head first onto concrete out of a lifted truck. Everyone of these involved hitting my head. That makes me sound clumsy but I'm not clumsy. Accidents happen. Each of these accidents contributed to me not being able to see Dr. Brimhall's light and not being able to track an object coming towards me such as a ball. No one knows for sure if I was born with a brain imbalance or if the concussions caused it, but over the years, I've found the answers I needed for my health—and for my patients, too. If I don't know how to help someone, I won't stop until I find a way. I am grateful to God that He kept bringing me answers one by one for each of my life's health challenges and for my patients.

People have told me, "Oh, I saw stars after that hit..." Or, "I only blacked out for a few seconds..." Or, "I couldn't remember anything about those few hours after I got hit..." Every one of these situations is a concussion.

Concussions spread out from the area of impact on the brain like spider webs. The effects are not just something for that moment. They create life-long consequences. Think about Mohammad Ali. He is one of the extreme cases. But, every hit has an effect on the brain to some degree.

NEW "ROADS" TO MENTAL HEALTH

For me, learning didn't come easily. I had to work three times as hard as others to retain information. I couldn't sit still. I was always moving and squirming. I remember my mom grabbing my hands and putting them in my lap and telling me, "Just sit still."

Well, I couldn't sit still.

As it turns out, I'm a kinetic learner, which means I need to be moving to focus, whether playing with something in my hands or doodling. If I can draw while listening to a teacher I am focused on what that person is saying. But, if I have to just sit there my mind drifts off and I day dream or think about lots of other things and I miss pretty much everything that is being said. I also wondered if I might have dyslexia, especially since some of my grandchildren do. That curiosity led me to study neurology, and now I help people with dyslexia, ADHD/ADD, OCD, Parkinson's, dementia, Alzheimer's, autism, and other neurological disorders.

Our brains are fascinating, marvelously created by God. We still know so little about how that organ, our brain, orchestrates everything within our neural pathways. Through neuroplasticity, our brains even allow us to build new "roads" if part of the brain is damaged—whether from a concussion or a brain deficit.

Working with a strong-willed child who has autism or dyslexia is hard work. They can experience violent outbursts when attempting tasks that would be simple for you and me. But to them, these tasks feel overwhelming.

I remember one sweet little girl pressing her head in her hands and saying, "My brain! My brain! I'm trying to make it do what I want, but it won't!"

Her brain was struggling to process information without a clear neuropathway. Watching the tears and tantrums can be heartbreaking. But we do difficult things to help each child reach their fullest potential.

One very proud little girl once shared her progress with me, "Dr. Cindy, it used to take me forty-five minutes or more to stop the rage tantrum in my brain. I would try and try to make my brain stop, but it wouldn't. Now that I've been coming to see you, I finally made my brain stop raging in less than fifteen minutes."

She was so proud of herself, and she should have been. She put in the work, alongside her family, to develop the weaker side of her brain. This precious girl has made significant improvements because we first tested to find out what parts of her brain were underdeveloped, then created a plan to help her build new "roads" and create new neural pathways. It didn't happen overnight. It took time and repetition to forge new paths in the brain. But it was worth it, leading to a healthier, better-functioning brain that created a happier life for the child and everyone around them.

REBUILDING, LAYER BY LAYER

Through it all, God has connected me with brilliant teachers—many of them experts in neurology and believers in Jesus Christ. They're humbled by God's greatness and acknowledge that as much as we know, there's still so much more to discover.

What keeps me going is the drive to help those who feel lost—the people who've seen every doctor and tried every treatment and still feel trapped in their bodies. They come to me saying, "My blood work and tests all look fine. The doctors can't find anything wrong with me." Some have even been told by their doctors, "It's all in your head."

I remember one instance when my son called. He knew he had a real problem, but the doctors couldn't figure it out. He had been medically discharged from the Marine Corps with an 80% disability. His wife explained that the VA had spent $50,000 that summer on tests, trying to figure out what was wrong. He couldn't remember his wife's name or how to get home.

He described his experience: "I have a test...I need a pencil. Okay. I have a pencil...I have a test...I need a pencil." He would get stuck in an endless loop in his mind, unable to break free. He was in severe pain all over his body and couldn't sleep.

I knew he had Lyme disease, but the VA wouldn't consider it. After three weeks of natural treatment, he could think clearly again. He wasn't entirely well after just three weeks—Lyme requires more time—but he had made significant progress.

That's the reality of wellness care—it's about rebuilding, layer by layer. It takes time, patience, and commitment. Medical care might offer a quick band-aid, but natural, lasting healing comes when you invest in the process. It's not just the physical body that needs healing, either. Emotions play a critical role. Trauma has a way of embedding itself deep within us, manifesting as physical symptoms, chronic conditions, or emotional blocks we're not even aware of.

This is where Neuro-Emotional Technique (N.E.T.) has been life-changing for my patients and me. N.E.T. helps people work through their emotional trauma, removing the "sting" of those experiences so they can finally live without the weight of their past. We all carry baggage from our past, from disappointments and traumas. When some doctors tell their patients that their problems are "all in their head," to some extent, they may be right.

Life can be harsh, and the emotions formed from painful experiences often manifest as symptoms of "dis-ease." This dis-ease, or heartbreak, expresses itself in a person's weakest physical area. If the lungs are vulnerable, they may develop bronchitis or asthma; if the stomach is weak, they may suffer from acid reflux; if the intestines are affected, they may experience

Crohn's disease or irritable bowel syndrome. A starving brain may lead to depression. Research shows that N.E.T. can improve the brain by alleviating the emotional impact of past experiences, allowing people to live their best lives.

It doesn't mean what happened to you was okay, but N.E.T. can help you face the hard things and find healing. You might even want to look up the *Grey's Anatomy* episode that featured Neuro-Emotional Technique—it's a fun watch. I love this technique because it's a life-changer for my patients.

A BASIS IN FAITH

All the training, techniques, and degrees I've earned are invaluable, but they're not what truly matters in my work. The real key has always been my faith. Every day, I pray for my patients, asking God to guide me, to give me wisdom, and to bless each of them with exactly what they need. It's a quiet moment of surrender, a reminder that I'm not alone in carrying the weight of their care.

So, what am I good at? It's simple—I genuinely care about people. My heart's deepest desire is to help them heal, to see them made whole. And through my struggles, faith has been the foundation that's kept me grounded.

Looking back, I realize how much of this strength was planted in me early on. My parents took us to church, and there I found a love for music that lifted my spirit. Singing in the choir and playing instruments filled me with joy, and the piano became my refuge. The hymns especially brought me peace—each note, a reminder that there's something bigger, a grace that holds us through every season.

In the end, that's what helped me put my life back together; a faith that never let go, even when everything else seemed to be falling apart.

I have loved Jesus for as long as I can remember. I accepted Christ in sixth grade, sitting under the big, open sky at the Circle-C Ranch, listening to John Ankerberg with Kansas City Youth For Christ. From that moment on, I was all in. In junior and senior high, I led Bible studies and wore my faith openly, even though it made me stand out and earned me plenty of teasing. But the name-calling and awkward stares couldn't shake me; I had a purpose that ran deeper than the everyday struggles of fitting in.

What mattered most to me was that the people I loved—my family, cousins, and friends—knew the peace and promise of salvation. I wanted them to know Jesus as I did, to have the assurance of something eternal, something unbreakable. Looking back now, I see how that mission has been the thread running through everything I've done. Degrees, career achievements, accolades— they're all just noise in comparison to the call to share Jesus' love.

If you're holding your own pieces and wondering where to go from here, maybe take a moment to ask: what's the purpose that pulls you forward, even on the hardest days? For me, it's been sharing a love that heals, redeems, and never lets go. And I hope, whatever it is for you, it's something that fills you with the strength to keep moving forward, one step at a time.

As you sit here, taking a moment to look back on the journey you've traveled, you might find yourself wondering about the strength that helped you through. Perhaps you're searching for something deeper, something that gives meaning to the struggles, the rebuilding, and the hopes that now seem within reach.

If you're ready to open your heart, to let go of the past, and to seek a love that endures beyond life's twists and turns, consider this: God's love is here, waiting for you. No matter the broken pieces you carry, His love has the power to make you whole again.

Take heart in the promise: "For I know the plans I have for you, declares the Lord, plans to prosper you and not to harm you, plans to give you hope and a future" (Jeremiah 29:11).

This journey, filled with hope and resilience, is just beginning.

"For God so loved the world, that He gave His only begotten Son, that whoever believes in Him shall not perish, but have eternal life" (John 3:16). This love offers healing, forgiveness, and the strength to move forward.

All you need to do is ask.

DR. CINDY STEWARD

With a passion for holistic healing and decades of experience, Dr. Cindy Steward uses the wisdom of being a Naturopathic doctor to transform lives. Dr. Steward holds dual Bachelor of Science degrees in Biology and Nutrition, providing a solid foundation for her holistic approach to wellness. Her approach incorporates cutting-edge techniques like neurological brain training for autism, Neuro-Emotional Technique (N.E.T.), quantum neurology, and many others. Each is a personalized treatment that addresses both physical and emotional health. Dr. Steward has trained under world-renowned experts such as Dr. Robert Melillo (Brain Balancing), Dr. George Gonzles (Quantum Neurology), Dr. Milton Dowty (CPK), deepening her expertise in cutting-edge neurological and functional medicine practices.

When she's not transforming lives through her practice, Dr. Steward finds joy and energy in her family. As a wife, mother, and grandmother, she cherishes the time spent with her loved ones.

www.OasisOfHealth.Healthcare

16

THE DIMMER SWITCH ISN'T WORKING

BY CARRIE KASS

From the moment I was born, life seemed determined to test my resilience. As the daughter of a young mother, with parents who divorced when I was just two years old, my childhood was far from conventional. Yet, even in those early years, a spark within me refused to be extinguished.

My early memories are a patchwork of time spent with my grandparents and weekly visits with my dad. This was my "normal," a concept that would be redefined multiple times throughout my life. Little did I know that these experiences were laying the foundation for a strength that would carry me through the storms to come.

A New Family, A New Identity

When I was eight, my world shifted dramatically. My mother remarried, and suddenly, I had a new dad who legally adopted me. With this came a new name and an entirely new family dynamic. The transition was jarring, to say the least. All contact with my biological father ceased, and I found myself navigating a completely unfamiliar landscape.

I don't recall any specific conversation as to why I would no longer see my birth dad. It didn't mean that there wasn't one. Perhaps I blocked it out to save my feelings. It was like I woke up the next day and was a new character in this movie of my life.

The awkwardness of this situation was amplified by the fact that my new dad was a teacher in my school district, and my mom occasionally substituted. Imagine the confusion and discomfort of coming to school one day with a new name and trying to explain it to classmates and teachers alike. It was as if I was expected to shed my old identity like a snake shedding its skin.

Despite the internal turmoil, I adopted a mindset of excellence. I was determined to be the best I could be—a responsible kid at home, a good student at school, and a leader in various activities. This drive for perfection was perhaps my way of seeking control in a situation where I felt I had none.

The new family I was thrust into was a stark contrast to what I had known. As an only child of an only child, I suddenly became the "oldest cousin" in a large, boisterous family. The sheer number of relatives at gatherings was overwhelming at first. Yet, their warmth and love quickly won me over, and I found myself embracing this new extended family.

The shock of this transition was immense, but my inner light refused to dim. Instead, it seemed to burn brighter, fueled by the challenge of adapting to my new circumstances.

The Unexpected Revelation

Fast forward to fifth grade, and life threw another curveball my way. A boy a year or two older than me approached me in the school hallway. His words hit me like a physical blow: "Hi, I'm [name]. Your dad and my mom got married, and he adopted me. So I guess we are kinda family".

The shock, anger, and grief that washed over me in that moment were indescribable. This innocent revelation opened up a world of questions and emotions I wasn't prepared to face. It was as if the ground beneath my feet had suddenly become unstable.

In the aftermath of this encounter, I made the decision to switch school districts. In my head, I was thinking, "Geez, it's already weird seeing my mom or dad in my school, but now I don't know what other "family" I have here!" I just wanted away from it all. I wanted a path that I could start walking on alone, a path I could control. It was a bold move for a young girl, but I was determined not to let this strange and uncomfortable situation dim my light. This was shock number two, but once again, the dimmer switch refused to work.

New Beginnings and Hidden Struggles

Starting sixth grade in a new school was challenging, especially at an age when girls are navigating the complex waters of friendship and identity. Yet, I powered through, making lifelong friends and creating beautiful high school memories. I excelled academically and took on the responsibilities of a latch-key kid, further shaping my independent and driven persona.

As I approached my senior year, my overachieving tendencies kicked into high gear. I was graduating top of my class and applying to some of the most prestigious schools in the country. Was I an overachiever? Absolutely. Was I looking for validation? Probably. But more than anything, I was determined to forge my own path, preferably one that led far away from Ohio.

The acceptance letters rolled in; Pepperdine, Duke, Wake Forest, Cornell, University of Michigan. Each one felt like a validation of my hard work and a ticket to a new life. However, reality soon set in as my mother and I sat down to review the financial packages. The dream schools were out of reach, and I found myself accepting a spot at Case Western Reserve University in Cleveland, Ohio – the last place I wanted to be.

This was shock number three. The disappointment was palpable, but I refused to let it dim my light. Little did I know how this seemingly disappointing turn of events would play a crucial role in shaping my future.

The Letter That Changed Everything

The summer after graduation brought another seismic shift in my world. A simple white envelope arrived in the mail, with no return address. Inside was a letter from my biological father—the man I had not seen or heard from since I was eight years old.

The contents of the letter unleashed a flood of emotions—confusion, anger, bewilderment, sadness, and grief. He wrote of his love for me, his pride in my achievements, how he had followed my accomplishments in the local newspaper. And that's when it hit me—the *local* newspaper. My father had been living less than thirty minutes away my entire life.

The realization was staggering. I had built walls around this part of my past, choosing not to dwell on it to protect myself. But now, those walls were crumbling, and I was faced with questions I wasn't sure I wanted answered. I approached my mother with a few cautious inquiries, but I didn't dig too deep. Self-preservation was still my primary instinct.

Remember when I changed schools because I wanted to embark on a path that I was in control of? The same held true. I did not want any part of digging up the past or having it in any way affect my life going forward.

This was shock number four. The dimmer switch flickered, but I stubbornly refused to let it dim my light. Instead, I channeled my energy into preparing for the next chapter of my life—college.

The Darkness That Threatened to Engulf Me

Freshman year at CWRU felt like a fresh start, a chance to reinvent myself away from the complications of my past. I threw myself into campus life, making friends, joining a sorority, and embracing the freedom of college life. I was determined to live life on my own terms, make my own choices, and forge my own destiny.

It was during this time that I met an art student who seemed to embody everything I found exciting about this new chapter in my life. Our connection was instant—great conversations, lots of laughs, and an undeniable attraction. One evening, he invited me to his dorm to show me an art project he had just finished.

What started as an exciting evening quickly turned into a nightmare. The details of what happened next are mercifully blurred in my memory, but the aftermath is crystal clear. I had been raped. The words "I don't want to," "Please let me go," and "You're hurting me" echoed in my head, battling with his responses of "You are the one who came to my room," "You'll be fine," "You know you want this," "We are so good together."

As I walked back to my dorm, I was already trying to rationalize what had happened. Was it my fault? Did I ask for this? The shame and confusion were overwhelming. I swore to myself that I would not let this dim my light, that I would simply avoid him on campus and move on with my life.

This was shock number five, and for the first time, the dimmer switch seemed to work. Though I didn't realize it at the time, this event changed me profoundly. I became reckless, partying more than I should have, and kissing more boys than I should have. I was searching for safety, security, and love in all the wrong places.

The Mask of Normalcy

In my junior year, I found what I thought was safety in a new relationship. This person seemed to understand me, having his own childhood traumas that we could bond over. It was with him that I experienced my first panic attack when I saw my "art guy" again after two years. For the first time, I opened up about what had happened to me, and I felt a sense of peace and safety.

This relationship became my anchor, especially when my mom and adopted dad divorced during my junior year of college. We stayed together through college and moved in together after graduation. I thought I had finally found stability and happiness.

But the truth was, I was simply putting on a mask. I was going through the motions of life, still deadened by what had happened but never really understanding or acknowledging it. We got married two years out of college, and I convinced myself that this was my happily ever after—a successful marriage, successful careers, a perfect life.

The Wedding Day Betrayal

As I planned my wedding, I wanted both my mom and my adopted dad to walk me down the aisle. Despite their divorce, I respected the man who had raised me and wanted him by my side on my special day.

When I called to share this with him, his response shattered me, "Carrie, I don't know if I'm coming to your wedding."

The shock, confusion, and anger were overwhelming. Those were the last words we ever spoke to each other. While most of his family showed up to support me, his absence left a gaping hole in what should have been one of the happiest days of my life.

Once again, I found myself disappointed by a man in my life, but I chose to pack away the pain and move on. The dimmer switch flickered, but the love and support of family turned it back on.

The Loss That Opened My Eyes

A few years into my marriage, I got pregnant. While I had never had a strong desire for children, it seemed like the next logical step in life. However, fate had other plans. At about seven weeks, I suffered a miscarriage.

The physical and emotional pain was unlike anything I had ever experienced. As I lay in the ER, surrounded by blood and tears, I felt completely lost. This traumatic event forced me to confront questions I had been avoiding for years. Did I really want to have a baby? Was this the life I wanted? Who was I, really?

As I grappled with these questions, my thoughts turned to my biological father. If I had had a child, he would never have known he was a grandfather. Did he deserve to know? Did he deserve a chance to make amends? The dimmer switch absolutely worked for a period of time, but I started turning it back on as I asked these questions.

The Reconnection That Changed Everything

In a moment of clarity, I decided to reach out to my aunt, asking her to give my number to my biological father. When he called, his first words —"Hi Carrie, this is your dad"—hit me like a ton of bricks. In the span of a thirty-minute conversation, I went from having no dad to having a heartfelt connection with the man I hadn't seen or spoken to in twenty-five years. To be honest, that conversation was one of two terrified people mumbling over words and not really knowing what to say or how to express it. After settling into it for a few minutes, I let him talk. And everything that came out was about love and regret. It made me want more.

Were there tears? You bet. So many emotions washed over me when I hung up. I had so many questions, questions that I did not want to ask over the phone; questions I needed answered.

Later that year, I met my dad, grandma, and aunt in person. The man I had resented, even hated at times, turned out to be one of the gentlest souls I had ever encountered. I could feel his love in every hug, every word. This reunion marked the beginning of my healing process, and the pieces of my life started to connect in ways I never imagined.

The End of a Chapter, The Beginning of Purpose

As I began to heal and grow, I realized that my marriage was falling apart. We were moving in different directions, wanting different things in life. When my husband said he wanted a divorce, I simply said "okay" and walked out the door. It was a bittersweet moment—filled with sadness and heartbreak, but also exhilaration and excitement for what the future might hold.

During this time of transition, I met John. Our connection was instant and profound. He saw something in me that I hadn't yet recognized in myself.

"You have a story to share," he told me. "I see you speaking to and leading women from your heart." His words planted a seed that would eventually grow into my purpose.

Finding My Light in Austin

Two years of dating John long-distance led to a decision to move to Austin, Texas together. This move marked the beginning of a new chapter in my life. I left a job of ten years, sold everything I owned minus personal belongings and my car, and took a twenty-four-hour, cross-country journey to my new city. Everything was brand new to me, and I was exhilarated and terrified all at the same time. It was all about taking the chance, stepping out on faith, and going for it.

In Austin, I also found a job I love, formed meaningful forever friendships, and started a women's empowerment networking group. And now, in the quest to continue to keep my light shining and to be a light for others, I'm sharing parts of me that aren't easy to share. Vulnerability is truly a beautiful space to come from, and for the first time, I feel like I am starting to truly live out my purpose.

What happened to John and I, you ask? John and I got married after ten years of dating, something neither of us thought we'd do again. Was it easy? No. Does the trauma of the past still rear its head? Of course. Is it where I know I'm supposed to be? 100%!

Being married to this man is part of my purpose. I believe that God had his hand on us and put us in the same place on His time. Perhaps neither John nor I were ready for the relationship at that point, but through God's persistent tap on our shoulders, here we are. This part of the story is its own chapter that maybe I'll share one day.

Looking back, I can now see how each piece of my life, even the painful ones, led me to where I am today. If I hadn't gone to CWRU, I wouldn't have experienced the trauma that shaped me. If I hadn't reconnected with my biological father, my heart might still be guarded. If I hadn't met John, I might not be in Austin, where life is forming up exactly as it is supposed to.

The Unbreakable Spirit

Through it all—the family upheavals, the betrayals, the trauma, the loss—my inner light refused to be dimmed. Each challenge, each setback, and each moment of pain only served to make that light burn brighter. I've always had the heart to lead, to connect people, to serve. Now, I'm living out my purpose, and I'm just getting started.

The journey from broken pieces to purpose hasn't been easy, but it's been profoundly transformative. My story is a testament to the resilience of the human spirit, the power of forgiveness, and the importance of staying true to oneself. The dimmer switch that life kept trying to use on me? It never worked. My light continues to shine, brighter than ever, illuminating not just my path, but hopefully the paths of others around me.

CARRIE KASS

Carrie Kass is a prominent healthcare leader serving as director of operations and business development at the Center for Healing and Regenerative Medicine (CHARM). Since opening CHARM in 2011, she has transformed it into a national leader in regenerative medicine through innovative strategies and clinical expertise.

As owner/director of Ladies Lifestyle Network Austin, Carrie leads a dynamic organization dedicated to women's empowerment and professional development. The network hosts monthly events featuring inspiring speakers and creates opportunities for women to connect with mentors, customers, and friends.

A sought-after connector and speaker in Austin, Carrie has held numerous leadership positions across state and national organizations.

Connect with Carrie:

LinkedIn: linkedin.com/in/carrie-kass-a59114a
Personal Facebook: facebook.com/carriekass18
Personal Instagram: @thecarriekass

ONE VERTEBRA AT A TIME

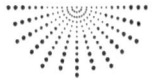

ANGELINA SMITH

*A*t six years old, I lay on my back with my feet propped on my bed, the orangish-yellow light of the lamp filling my bedroom. It had been another day of family fighting, and I needed an escape. My little pink radio played Amy Grant, and her melody wrapped around me, singing so vividly about seeing, feeling, and knowing God everywhere in the face of Jesus. It was personal. It was my heart song. Her words transported me, and God's loving embrace held my fragile heart, mind, and being. That moment sealed me with a purpose forever—to love and serve God, to do whatever was asked of me so I could stay close to that place with Him. The message was imprinted on the blueprint of my heart.

Before that, my sisters and I followed Mom from one church to another as she sought the right flavor of religion. We shuffled through Baptist, Methodist, Jehovah's Witnesses, and non-denominational until finally landing in Pentecostal. Sundays were an unpredictable string of worship events, like a small-town Texas jail-cell ministry, where my mom would lead praise with her "brother-in-the-Lord" while my sisters and I waited under a shade tree with sandwiches. Then, we'd be off to a Spanish-speaking service, where the preacher occasionally translated into English when she remembered.

Meanwhile, my dad worked constantly—he was an auto mechanic and tow truck driver—and was never home, not even on holidays. The only times I recall my parents in the same room were when they were arguing. His frequent refrain was "Get a job," to which she'd preach back, urging him to "get saved."

Mama made the best food. Her being home meant warm, savory meals, always complemented by flour tortillas. She could pull together a full meal when I swore nothing was in the fridge. I didn't realize what a gift that was.

Later, I'd appreciate it when dinners with Dad was a frozen Night Hawk or, on Mondays, Hamburger Helper—the closest we got to a home-cooked meal.

As kids, we grew accustomed to hearing Mom belt out praise songs in Spanish and English while getting ready for school or being schlepped from one vacation Bible school to the next. Her loud alto voice was as much a part of our mornings as the discipline that could come at any moment: the belt, the shoe, or the hanger.

By thirteen, my parents divorced. I was old enough to choose between them but couldn't. The judge awarded custody to Dad because he had a job.

I gravitated toward church, mimicking every action and ritual—dancing until my shoes came off, falling on the floor, speaking in tongues, attending five a.m. prayer meetings, and regularly fasting. They said it, I did it. I quickly learned that performing these activities brought attention, affection, and acceptance—the only place I could get it. Mom's visits dwindled, which hurt deeply, and when Dad was around, he preferred making jokes at our expense over true engagement.

One day, a kind man approached me at work, whispering, "I heard you're a believer."

I smiled back and nodded.

Soon, his son began showing up "to see his dad." As the receptionist, I was the first person he saw. His hazel eyes, slightly downturned, also gave the impression that he needed care and affection. His voice was deep and raspy, his love for God so genuine that he read the Bible on lunch breaks and wrote poems for the Lord that melted my heart. I fell quickly.

We were engaged after just two months when he held me close and said he couldn't imagine life without me. I left my broken home and sped to a slower life in the country, where his parents were still married, could sit together lovingly, and led worship at church. I thought I was positioned to live happily ever after. I had a man who loved Jesus. What else was there?

I quit college, and we both landed jobs at the phone company; he was a line installer, and I worked in customer service. With steady paychecks, we bought a brand-new starter home, and soon, I was driving a forest-green Ford

Mustang with tan leather seats, a car he'd bought for me.

The funny thing was, I didn't know a thing about cars or how to dream about what kind of car I wanted, much less how to speak up about anything.

I kept up my people-pleasing behavior, smiling and going along to get along. Soon, he got a new truck, and we launched into a lifestyle of spending before we earned it. I also began seeing his short-fused temper, which hadn't shown itself during our courtship.

I remember thinking, *If I could handle Dad's outbursts, I can handle his.*

And I did. I tried to manage life so as not to set him off. If I didn't understand something, I buried it. When he wanted to spend money we didn't have or go out with friends, I nodded and smiled. I didn't know how to name my emotions, much less express them.

On November 14, 2002, we had our beautiful, perfect daughter—our Valentine's baby. He hadn't been ready to be a father, but that February night, he allowed God's will, and soon, we knew it was God's will that we had a child. She became my world. I was obsessed with ensuring she knew unconditional love and would never know abandonment. Each night, after battling my commute home, I poured myself into our few precious evening hours. But it began to take a toll on our marriage, which grew cold and brittle. I built up walls around our daughter and I effectively shutting him out. He spent more time with friends, consumed with adrenaline-fueled hobbies, including cars, trucks, and motorcycles. He rebuilt a silver Mustang to "sound angry," then traded it for a Corvette.

I dog-paddled through life, disconnected from myself. My heart and sense of self stayed divided, and I didn't know how to bridge them. I didn't know how to deal with my dissatisfaction or the feeling that I wasn't enough to keep him home. I let him go, focusing instead on my time with our daughter. My identity as a wife crumbled internally, while outwardly, I clung desperately to my "happy wife" image, holding it together with sheer will. It's how I earned the title of "Ice Queen." During this time, I allowed myself to savor the attention of other men.

One Tuesday morning, on my first day as an account manager, I received a fruit bouquet—the kind I love, with food displayed as art. I assumed it was from my husband. But when I read the card, my world spun.

Your husband has not been faithful.

The delivery stunned me. I called him, but he brushed it off, claiming the woman who sent it was crazy. I couldn't process what I felt or even begin to name the emotions I needed to express. So, I threw the bouquet away and went back to work, holding onto the belief that my marriage was the lovely Christian one I had envisioned. Divorce wasn't an option. I had vowed I would not have a marriage like my parents.

When our daughter was two, I became pregnant again. At our first sonogram, they discovered our baby had a "halo" around her head. I thought it meant she was angelic, but the doctors diagnosed her with hydrocephalus. She wouldn't survive. Yet, week after week, she continued to grow and showed strength. I hoped for a miracle, believing God might heal her. But at six months, I felt a change. I delivered her with two pushes, and, wanting to remember her as perfect, I chose not to see her. My husband did, and it broke him. Our shared grief was confined to that moment in the hospital parking lot.

In the weeks following, I savored time with our toddler, grateful for the leave that allowed me to enjoy walks, playground visits, and shared meals. But I didn't use that time to grieve; I didn't know how.

One sunny day, I met my best girlfriend for lunch and did something I'd never done before. After we'd eaten chips and queso, I looked her in the eye and said, "I feel lost. It's like I've been given the script for a happy, Christian life, and I've done my best to follow it, but inside, I hurt, and I don't even know why. I can't find the words to match what I feel."

My friend didn't judge me. She held my gaze and listened. Her skillful blend of compassion and nosy curiosity was precisely what I needed. She gave me a safe place to be myself. That moment ushered in a new phase in my life—a time of talking, sharing, and experimenting with what it felt like to be honest about myself and my struggles instead of editing my image to match expectations.

Not long after, I went on a girls' trip with two dear Christian friends I'd met at work. We wanted to see what Chip and Joanna Gaines had done with the Silos in Waco. Over coffee and pastries, I unloaded the current edition of my woes and was immediately told, "You need to go to Al-Anon."

I'd never heard of it, but her directive was clear, and I was desperate enough to follow it. I immediately found a newcomer meeting and visited, amazed to see people living with loved ones in the throes of addiction while handling it with genuine, palpable faith. This faith stood firm even in the face of indescribable adversities.

The faith I encountered there was unlike the on-and-off, performance-based experience I'd known in my relationship with God. Until then, my understanding of God had been shaped by trying to earn His favor, hoping my good behavior would yield the promised blessings. Yet, I'd done "all the right things," and life still felt hollow. I couldn't reconcile why the math didn't add up. I had been the good girl. I'd kept praying, kept trying to please, but my life wasn't what I'd hoped. Where had I gone wrong?

I spent my first few meetings in tears, learning to let go of the polished cover I'd been hiding behind. I practiced a ruthless authenticity and discovered that God was not the taskmaster I'd imagined. He was compassionate, patient, and true, big enough to handle all my insecurities, fears, and ignorance. The lack of knowledge wouldn't hold me back. I realized that if I were willing, He would grow me beyond it. I had to unlearn my performance-based approach to God.

Early on, I also learned that I didn't understand true forgiveness. I had taken it to mean "seventy times seven," as in Matthew 18:21-22—that is, every time. I believed that forgiveness meant swallowing every injustice, smiling through it, and burying it all under forced cheerfulness. But as reality settled in, I saw that what I'd been calling forgiveness was actually denial. I'd been sweeping things under the rug, gritting my teeth, and weakly smiling as though nothing hurt. Coming to terms with this truth was painful. I spent a long time grappling with what forgiveness really looked like.

I sought answers in books, sermons, and prayer, but nothing reached where I was. I came to see that forgiveness wasn't about pretending everything was okay. Instead, it was about acknowledging the wrongs done, naming my feelings, and bringing them to God. Only He could heal the hurt. He saw the whole picture, and His justice could be trusted. Forgiveness also meant setting boundaries—holding people accountable—so that if the same wrong happened again, I could say, "I love you, but this is not okay." In these small moments of honesty, I grew a backbone, one vertebra at a time.

Life kept moving. I attended my daughter's gymnastics lessons, Girl Scouts, and cheerleading practices. Her dad would show up for the photos but would soon leave to meet up with friends. He was there—but only halfway.

Despite marriage counseling and individual therapy, we eventually divorced after almost eighteen years. We drew up the paperwork ourselves—we didn't have money for lawyers—and began the sixty-day waiting period, which stretched into a year as we made one last attempt to work things out.

One late Tuesday night, he came home tipsy from a night out with friends. He had broken plans for dinner with his parents, and I stayed awake so he could see my face. As he climbed the stairs, I prayed, searching for the right words. What came out was, "What do you have to say for yourself?" But as he answered, I realized his words no longer mattered. The door had closed on us, and nothing he could say would reopen it.

After amicably drawing up divorce paperwork from the online law library, we discussed going before the judge to finalize things. He insisted he'd go with me, but on that Monday morning, when I presented my case, I was alone—but I stood with my spine intact.

Afterward, I had a brief fling but was soon ghosted, and everything came crashing down. That year, the old me died. I spent the year in mourning, like someone who'd finally let go of the dam, allowing all the unprocessed hurt, trauma, and grief to flood out. During those dark days, I couldn't understand what the point of anything was. My days felt foggy, as if I moved through them in slow motion. I felt nothing—no highs, no lows. I was numb.

I put one foot in front of the other, journaled, cried, prayed, went to counseling and Al-Anon meetings, and walked around the lake with friends, sorting through the mess of my emotions.

Then, one day, I made it through without crying. I noticed that my tear-stained glasses had dried, and I could finally take a deep, full breath. The sun, the sky, the birds, and the trees were beautiful again, and their beauty began to heal my soul. In that dark year, I learned how to position myself in safe spaces where God flowed freely. In His gentle, loving way, He healed my heart, piece by piece, moment by moment.

The feeling I'd experienced as a little girl in my bedroom began to bloom again. My hard-won lesson was simple; let go. Submit my will, my fears, and my hopes to Him. Stay open to the Holy Spirit's guidance; He will be with me everywhere I go.

Today, I'm married to a lovely man with a heart of gold. I gained two bonus daughters and a son-in-law, making a family of four children, with talks of grandbabies on the horizon. Our lives are full and blessed. When challenges come, I face them with a strong backbone, a vibrant heart, and a seasoned mind. I process openly with my girlfriends and the Lord, ready for new adventures and eager to follow the Holy Spirit into the unknown. Wherever He leads, I will follow.

ANGELINA SMITH

Angelina Smith is a native Texan born on the fourth of July and navigating life as a leftie. She lives in Georgetown with her husband. They have three grown daughters, two cats and an Aussiedoodle who makes regular appearances in family photos. Her passions include heart-to-heart talks on Saturday morning walks at the park with said pup, book clubs, Bible Study and a newfound adventure of narrating books on Audible! Her creativity has burst into her twenty plus year career at AT&T in the form of Ted Talk videos, interviews and Culture Chats for the local organization. She is positioning her life to leave a legacy of hope, passion and purpose to those in her sphere of influence. Author of "From Chaos to Clarity: 7 Steps for Applying Wisdom to Life's Journey on Instagram @Angelina_Reads_78

CENTRAL TEXAS TABLE OF GRACE

*A*ll proceeds from this multi-author book are donated to Central Texas Table of Grace.

Central Texas Table of Grace is a 501(c)(3) non-profit organization that exists to provide emergency shelter services to the foster children and administers our Grace365 Supervised Independent Living program for young adults aging out of foster care. Their support contributes to an improved quality of life for youth and their families. The organization's projects, implemented by an experienced staff, emphasize creating a caring climate for youth. Supporting the development of self-confidence, healthful living, and good judgment, Central

Texas Table of Grace provides our children with a thorough foundation for success.

Follow us on social media to find out more.

https://www.facebook.com/centraltexastableofgrace

https://www.instagram.com/ctxtableofgrace/

https://www.linkedin.com/company/central-texas-table-of-grace/

https://twitter.com/CTXTableOfGrace

https://www.tiktok.com/@ctxtableofgrace